Moza

Berchtesgadener Land and
Chiemgau

An original *cycline* guide

Esterbauer

cycline guide Mozart Bike Trail
© 2005, **Verlag Esterbauer GmbH**
A-3751 Rodingersdorf, Hauptstr. 31
Tel.: ++43/2983/28982
Fax.: ++43/2983/28982-500
E-Mail: bikeline@esterbauer.com
www.esterbauer.com
1st Edition, 2005

ISBN 3-85000-192-X

Please quote edition and ISBN number in all correspondence.

We wish to thank all the people who contributed to the production of this book, and especially: Gerd and Monika Morschhäuser, Winnenden; René Giesler; Eberhard Bremicker, Poppenricht; Hans Niederbuchner, Freilassing; Dr. Erwin Steinbauer, Enns; Karl E. Schmidt, Seelze-Velber; Wolfgang Kling, Fam. Müller, Tuttlingen; Kerstin Ines Kuhn, Gilching; Peter Rottensteiner, Salzburg; Gabi Scheil, Bad Reichenhall; Heinz Erath, Schramberg; Bernhard Adamski, Landau; V. Hofmann; Felicitas Riede, Freiburg; Rainer Vogt, Ganderkesee; Werner Schulte, Meinerzhagen; Andreas Bönki, Velen; Charlotte Kann, Nürnberg; Helga and Karl Herzog, Wien;

The *cycline* team: Birgit Albrecht, Beatrix Bauer, Grischa Begaß, Karin Brunner, Anita Daffert, Michaela Derferd, Roland Esterbauer, Maria Galbruner, Jutta Gröschel, Dagmar Güldenpfennig, Carmen Hager, Karl Heinzel, Veronika Loidolt, Michael Manowarda, Niki Novak, Maria Pfaunz, Andreas Prinz, Jenny Reisinger, Petra Riss, Martha Siegl, Matthias Thal. Translated from German by Otto Mayr.

Picture credits: VV Kufstein: Cover, Salzburger Land: 6; Tourismus Salzburg GmbH: 12, 14; Tourismusverband Eugendorf: 16; FVV St. Gilgen: 22; Tourismusverban Mondseeland-Weinhäupl: 25; Foto Költringer: 26; Salzburger Seenland Tourismus GmbH: 30, 32; Tourismusverband Anthering: 34; FVV Oberndorf: 36; FVV Laufen: 38; Tourismusbüro Teisendorf: 39; Inzeller Touristik GmbH: 40, 44; Veronika Loidolt: 52, 54, 58, 60, 62, 76, 84, 86, 91, 96, 98, 102; Tourist-Information Breitbrunn am Chiemsee: 60; Urlaub auf demBauernhof Chiemsee-Wendelstein: 62; Verkehrsamt Eggstätt: 64; H. Rupp: 64; Stadt Wasserburg/Inn: 66; Archiv: 72; Verkehrsamt Kiefersfelden: 78; Kur- und Verkehrsamt Oberaudorf: 80; Tourismusverband Mondseeland: 82; Tourismus Salzburg GmbH: 106, 108

Preface

Salzkammergut, Chiemgau and Tyrol. These three regions along the Austrian-German border dazzle with stunning landscapes, verdant Alpine pastures, meadows filled with wildflowers, crisp clean air and refreshing lakes. They are also popular vacation destinations and have an abundance of small roads perfect for bicycling. The lively city of Salzburg, hometown to Wolfgang Amadeus Mozart, offers an outstanding base from which to explore these regions. The Mozart Bike Trail connects Salzburg with the three famous regions and leads to many of the places that figured in the life of the 18th century musical genius: St. Gilgen on the Wolfgangssee, the Chiemsee, Waging and Wasserburg on the river Inn, to name just a few of the places where Mozart spent time. May a bicycle tour through Mozart's backyard be as relaxing as he found them to be in his lifetime!

This bicycle touring guide includes detailed maps of the countryside and of many cities and towns, precise route descriptions, information about historic and cultural sites as well as background information and a comprehensive list of overnight accommodations. The one thing this guide cannot provide is fine cycling weather, but we hope you encounter nothing but sunshine and gentle tailwinds.

Map legend

(The following colour coding is used:

———— main cycle route

———— cycle path / main cycle route without motor traffic

———— excursion or alternative route

.... planned cycle path

The surface is indicated by broken lines:

———— paved road

— — — — unpaved road

Routes with motor traffic are indicated by dotted lines:

• • • • • • cycle route with moderate motor traffic

• • • • • • cycle route with heavy motor traffic

• • • • • • cycle lane

road with heavy motor traffic

——➤ steep gradient, uphill

——➤ light gradient

⌐3⌐ distance in km

➤ cycle route direction

Scale 1 : 50.000
1 cm ≙ 500 m   1 km ≙ 2 cm

Schönern   picturesque town

( )   facilities available

hotel, guesthouse; youth hostel

camping site; simple tent site

tourist information; shopping facilities

restaurant; resting place

outdoor swimming pool; indoor swimming pool

buildings of interest

Mill   other place of interest

museum; theatre; excavation

zoo; nature reserve

panoramic view

P   parking lot; garage

boat landing; ferry

bike workshop; bike rental

covered ~; lockable bike stands

---

church; chapel; monastery

castle; ruins

tower; TV/radio tower

power station; transformer

windmill; windturbine

+× wayside cross; peak

mine

monument

sports field

airport, airfield

natural spring; waste water treatment plant

⚠ ⚠ dangerous section; read text carefully

stairs; narrow pass, bottleneck

X X X road closed to cyclists

in city maps:

post office; pharmacy

fire-brigade; hospital

---

0   1   2   3   4   5   6   7   8   9   10 km

~~	international border
⊖	border checkpoint
~~	country border
	forest
	rock, cliff
	marshy ground
	vineyard
	cemetary
	shallows
	dunes
	meadows
	embankment, dyke
	dam, groyne, breakwater
═══	motorway
───	main road
───	minor road
	carriageway
───	footpath
	road under construction
─▣─	railway with station
─▪▫▪─	narrow gage railway
	tunnel; bridge

Contents

The Mozart Bike Trail

The Mozart Bike Trail through the Salzkammergut and Chiemgau starts and ends in Salzburg, the Austrian city on the Salzach River where Wolfgang Amadeus Mozart was born on January 27, 1756. Mozart was a child prodigy and musical genius who could play the piano at the age of three, the violin when he was four, and who had already composed three operas, 6 symphonies and many other pieces by the time he was 12 years old.

Even as a child he traveled far and often gave concerts in the palaces and castles of European nobility. As a result, the relatively little time he spent in Salzburg and the surrounding regions were often like vacations. Those vacations were spent in places like the Chiemgau and the Salzkammergut, where he could visit friends and relatives and recover from the rigors of his travel schedule.

5

The Mozart Bike Trail leads from Salzburg to St. Gilgen in the Chiemgau to Tyrol and back to Salzburg.

About the cycling route

Length

The Mozart Bike Trail covers a total distance of about 431.5 kilometers, not including side trips or possible detours from the main route.

Road surface and traffic

Most of the Mozart Bike Trail follows quiet country lanes and paved farming and forestry

paths. Dedicated bicycle trails have been built along many of the rivers and lakes. Only a few short stretches follow unpaved roads, for instance near Roitham on the Chiemsee or the sidetrip to Reit im Winkel near Inzell. Traffic is almost always very light with the exception of several sections that are never longer than one or two kilometers. During busy periods heavier

traffic can be expected on the main Bundesstraße near Kirchdorf.

Signage

The entire Mozart Bike Trail from Salzburg to Rosenheim and back is marked with signs visible from both riding directions. Also posted with the distinctive signs bearing the image of Wolfgang Amadeus Mozart are the excursion route to St. Gilgen, the route from Laufen to Reit im Winkl and the alternative route through the Saalach valley. Signs in the Salzburger Land are

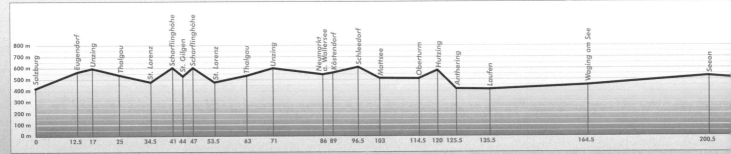

white with green lettering. Elsewhere they are white with brown lettering. Some sections may not always be posted with an optimum number of signs to guarantee easy orientation.

Planning your tour

Important telephone numbers

International dialing code for Austria: 0043. For Germany: 0049.

Tourism information sources

Salzburger Land Tourismus,
A-5300 Hallwang, ✆ 0662/6688-0,
E-Mail: info@salzburgerland.com;
www.salzburgerland.com

Tourismusverband Chiemgau,
D-83276 Traunstein, ✆ 0861/58333;
E-Mail: info@chiemgau-tourismus.de;
www.chiemgau-tourismus.de

Erlebnisregion Berchtesgadener Land,
D-83458 Schneizlreuth, ✆ 08665/7489;
E-Mail: info@bgl-rupertiwinkel.de; www.bgl-rupertiwinkel.de

Arrival and Departure by air

Salzburg's international airport – Salzburg Airport W.A. Mozart – is served by many major European commercial airlines, including Lufthansa, KLM, Air Lingus, Ryanair, and Aeroflot.

Arrival and Departure by rail

Salzburg is connected to other European countries by a large number of international InterCity and EuroCity passenger trains as well as regional lines. The city lies on Austria's main east-west line. Trains from Vienna arrive at the train station every half hour. Trains from major German cities arrive hourly.

Information:

Deutsche Bahn AG, **DB Information,** ✆ 11861 (Reservations, schedules and fares; 1.33 €/Min.), **DB Information** (no charge) ✆ 0800/1507090, www.bahn.de

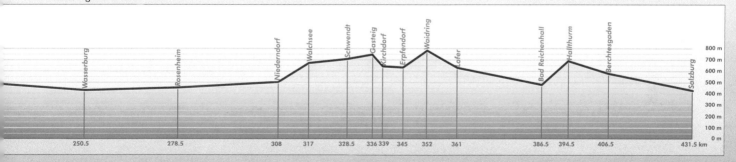

Deutsche Bahn AG, Bicyclist **Hotline** ☎ 01805/151415 (Mon-Fri 8-20, Sat and Sun 9-14; 0.12 €/Min.), additional information also at www.bahn.de/pv/uebersicht/die_bahn_und_bike.shtml

Österreichische Bundesbahnen (Austrian Rail), ÖBB-Schedules ☎ 05/1717, www.oebb.at

Bicycle transport

Bicycle transport on trains:

Germany: Train passengers may bring bicycles onto all trains identified with the 🚲 bike symbol in rail timetables, if the passenger purchases a bicycle ticket and there is sufficient space available on the train. A reservation for the bicycle is required on many inter-city trains, but not on regional trains.

Taking a bicycle on the train in Germany costs € 8, Bahncard holders pay € 6. The price on regional trains is € 3. Bicycles with trailers, tandems, recumbents, tri-cycles and motorized bicycles require the purchase of two bicycle tickets.

The bicycle reservation is free of charge and can be booked at the ticket counter or using the Radfahrer-Hotline (Tel: ☎ 01805/151415). Further information about connections, schedules and fares is also available by calling the Deutsche Bahn customer service number ☎ 01805/996633.

Austria: Train passengers in Austria may bring bicycles only onto trains identified with the 🚲 or (🚲) bike symbols in the rail timetables. The second symbol indicates that bicycles are permitted only during the following times: Mon-Fri 9-15 and after 18:30, Sat after 9, Sun/Hol all day. One must purchase a bicycle ticket and there must be sufficient space for bicycles on the train. Prices for bicycle tickets in Austria:

One-day bike ticket:	€ 2.90
One-week bike ticket:	€ 6.50
One-month bike ticket:	€ 19.60
One-year bike ticket:	€ 156.90

An international bicycle ticket costs € 10.20.

Bike & Rail along the bicycle route

It is also possible to switch to a train for certain stretches along the Mozart Bike Trail. For instance, one can take a train from Salzburg directly to Straßwalchen, to Laufen, or for the segment between Laufen and Freilassing. It is also possible to take the train along the Inn river from Wasserburg to Niederndorf. In the Tyrol region there are no train connections along the cycle route until one reaches Bad Reichenhall, were one can catch rail connections to Salzburg or Berchtesgaden.

For further information contact the Deutsche Bahn Radfahrer-Hotline: ☏ 01805/151415 or the ÖBB Call-Center ☏ 05/1717.

Accommodations

It is rarely difficult to find overnight accommodations along the route. A large number of hotels, inns, and campgrounds as well as private homes offering rooms can be found in Salzkammergut, Chiemgau, along the Inn river, in Tyrol and in the areas around Bad Reichenhall and Berchtesgaden. During peak vacation periods it is recommended that one

make reservations in advance, especially in the most popular summertime vacation areas like Salzkammergut and around the Chiemsee and in Tyrol.

Touring with small children

The Mozart Bike Trail is suitable for children over the age of 12 who have average physical condition and some experience riding bicycles on public roads. Most of the route follows quiet minor roads or paved farming and forestry service roads. Traffic is almost always light. There are a number of moderately difficult climbs.

The right bicycle

Any bicycle equipped with a good range of gears will suffice for the Mozart Bike Trail, though touring and trekking bicycles will provide the most comfort.

Regardless of what kind of bicycle one takes, we strongly recommend bringing basic tools and repair equipment. A complete tool kit should include a spare inner tube, patch kit, air pump, tire irons and wrenches as well as brake and shifter cables, a screwdriver, chain oil, rags and replacement light bulbs.

About this book

This bicycle touring guide contains all the information that you should need for a bicycling vacation along the Mozart Bike Trail: precise maps, a detailed description of the route, numerous detail maps of cities and towns, a comprehensive list of overnight accommodations, and information about important historic sites and other tourist attractions.

And all this information comes with the **cycline** guarantee: Every meter of the route described in this book has been tested and evaluated in person by one of our editors!

The maps

The inside of the guide's front cover shows an overview of the greater region covered by the guide. It also depicts the area shown by each of the detail maps inside the guide. These maps are produced in a scale of 1 : 50,000 (1 centimeter = 500 meters). In addition to exactly describing the route, these maps also provide information about roadway quality (paved or unpaved), climbs (gentle or steep), distances, as well as cultural and tourist highlights.

Note that the recommended main route is always shown in red or purple, while alternative routes and excursions are shown in orange. The individual symbols used in the maps are described in the legend on page 4.

Route elevation graphic

The route elevation graphic on pages 6 and 7 provides an overview of the location of important towns and major ascents and descents along the route. The graphic only shows major changes in elevation, not every single small incline. Major climbs and descents are also indicated with arrows on the individual maps.

The text

The text consists primarily of detailed route descriptions. These are especially useful in populated areas. The descriptions follow the main recommended route. Key phrases about the route description are indicated with the symbol.

This main text is interrupted in places by passages describing alternative and excursion routes. These are printed on a light orange background.

To aid in orientation, the names of main towns and villages are printed in bold type. Important points of interest in towns and places are listed with addresses, telephone numbers and opening times. In large cities we have only included a limited selection of noteworthy sights.

Descriptions of the larger towns and cities, as well as historic, cultural and natural landmarks help round out the travel experience. These paragraphs are printed in italics to distinguish them from the route description.

You will also find paragraphs printed in purple or orange ink to help draw attention to special features:

Text printed in purple indicates that you must make a decision about how your tour shall continue. For instance, there may be an alternative route to another destination or the recommended route deviates from posted route markers.

Orange text suggests possible excursions to points of interest or recreational facilities that do not lie directly on the cycling route.

List of overnight accommodations

The last pages of this cycling guide provide a list of convenient hotels and guest houses in virtually every village or town along the route. This list also includes youth hostels (🏠) and campgrounds (⛺). For more details, please refer to page 109.

From Salzburg to Laufen

135.5 km

From Salzburg to Laufen

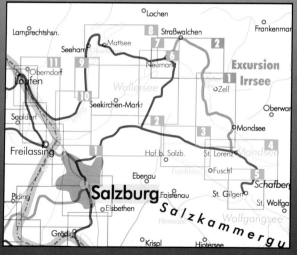

Salzburg: What could be a more appropriate starting point for the Mozart Bike Trail than the Austrian composer's place of birth? The first part of the tour passes into one of Austria's most famous vacation regions – the beautiful Salzkammergut. Explore idyllic small cities like St. Gilgen on the Wolfgangsee, Mondsee or Obertrum am Mattsee. Linger, relax or wait for creative inspiration in charming locales where Mozart once did the same.

This part of the Mozart Bike Trail follows the Salzkammergut bicycle route. Most of it goes along quiet farm and forestry service roads. Along the Salzach River the trail is packed gravel and in the Chiemgau one rides mainly along minor secondary roads. Traffic is light with the exception of a few short stretches on moderately busy roads. There are several climbs, especially in the hilly Salzkammergut.

11

Salzburg

Postal code: A-5020; Telephone area code: 0662

- **🅱 Tourist Information**, Auerspergstr. 6, ☏ 88987-0, Fax 88987-32
- **🅱 Information Hauptbahnhof**, Bahnsteig 2a, ☏ 88987-340
- **🅱 Information Mozartplatz**, Mozartpl. 5, 88987-330
- **🅱 Information Salzburg-Süd**, Park-and-Ride, ☏ 88987-360
- **🏛 Salzburg Baroque Museum**, Mirabellgarten, ☏ 877432, Open: Tues-Sat 9-12 and 14-17, Sun/Hol 10-13, European art from the 17th and 18th centuries
- **🏛 Toy Museum/Musical Instrument Museum**, Bürgerspitalg. 2, ☏ 620808-300, Open: Tues-Sun 9-17. Toy collection, arts and crafts, historical musical instruments
- **🏛 Salzburg Museum Carolino Augusteum**, Museumspl. 1, ☏ 620808-200, Open: Daily 9-17, Thurs 9-20. Art and cultural history of Salzburg and the region.
- **🏛 Cathedral archaeological museum**, Residenzplatz, ☏ 845295, Open: July and Aug 2004 daily 9-17, excavations from the medieval cathedral and Roman ruins.
- **🏛 Cathedral museum**, Cathedral foyer, ☏ 844189, Open: 7 May-31 Oct 2004, 20 Nov 2004-6 Jan 2005, Mon-Sat 10-17, Sun/Hol 11-18; Medieval to 19th century art belonging to the Archdiocese of Salzburg.
- **🏛 Haus der Natur**, Museumspl. 5, ☏ 842653, Open: daily 9-17, nature studies museum including aquarium, reptile zoo and space exploration hall.

Mirabell garden

- **🏛 Museum der Moderne Salzburg Rupertinum**, Wiener-Philharmoniker-G. 9, ☏ 8042-2541, Open: daily except Mon 10-18, Weds 19-21, during Festival weeks (Mozart Week, Easter, Summer) also open Mon 10-18; modern art, graphics, photography of the 20th and 21st centuries. The new Mönchsberg building of the **Museum der Moderne Salzburg** opened in October 2004.
- **🏛 Mozarts Geburtshaus**, Getreideg. 9, ☏ 844313, Open: daily 9-18, July/Aug daily 9-19; Mozart's birthplace and his family's home. Collection includes items from his life.
- **🏛 Mozarts Wohnhaus**, Makartpl. 8, Open: daily 9-18, July/Aug daily 9-19; Mozart's home, musical instruments.
- **🏛 Trachtenmuseum**, Griesg. 23/I, ☏ 843119, Open: Mon-Fri (workdays)10-12 and 14-17. Salzburg traditional folk costumes and dress.
- **🏛 Salzburger Freilichtmuseum**, Hasenweg, 5084 Großgmain, ☏ 850011, Open: 28 March-1 Nov, Tues-Sun 9-18, 26 Dec-6

Jan, daily 10-16. 50-hectare area at the foot of the Untersberg has 60 restored historic farmhouses from the 16th to 20th centuries.

- **⛪ Cathedral**, Dompl.; most monumental early baroque church north of the Alps.
- **⛪ St. Peter Abbey and catacombs**, ☏ 844578-0, Guided tours: May-Sept, Tues-Sun 10:30-17, Oct-April, Weds and Thurs 10: 30-15:30, Fri-Sun 10:30-16.
- **⛪ Fortress Hohensalzburg with castle museum**, Mönchsberg 34, ☏ 842430, Open: Fortifications and interior courtyards: 15 March-14 June, 9-18; 15 June-14 Sept, 9-19; 15 Sept-14 March, 9-17. Tour with audio guide in 7 languages (multi-visions show, defensive towers, prince's chambers, castle museum): 15 March-14 June, 9:30 –17:30; 15 June-14 Sept, 9-18; 15 Sept-14 March, 9:30-17. Reach castle by foot or take the cable car (see below). The largest fully-preserved castle in Europe. Built in 1077 and expanded over the centuries.
- **⛪ Residenz**, Residenzpl. 1; **Residenzgalerie**, Open: Tues-Thurs 10-17, 20 May-13 Jun 2004, 17 July-5 Sept 2004, 4 Dec-6 Jan. 2005: Open Mon; 1 Nov-26 Nov, 24 Dec 2004: Museum closed; European paintings from the 16th to 19th centuries. **Residenz chambers**, ☏ 8042/2690, Open: Jan-Dec, 10-17. Closed 1 Nov and 24 Dec 2004; Closed to public during special events! Residence of Salzburg's archbishops since 1120. Expanded in 1600 - 1619. Especially noteworthy are the magnificent interiors built 1709-1727 by Lukas von Hildebrandt as well as frescoes

and ceiling paintings by J.M. Rottmayr and M. Altomonte.

⑥ **Schloss Mirabell and Mirabell garden.** Marmorsaal (marble chamber) Open: Mon, Weds, Thurs, 8-16; Tues, Fri, 13-16. The palace was originally built in 1606 and redesigned by Lukas von Hildebrandt 1721-27. The garden contains groups of statues based on Greek mythology. Baroque angels' stairs: Open: daily 8-18. **Mirabell garden:** Open year-round, daily from about 6 to dark.

⑥ **Schloss Hellbrunn.** Manneristic early baroque summer residence with fountains. Guided tours only. Waterworks and folklore museum. Tours every 30 minutes, audio-guide, April, Oct 9-16:30, May, June, Sept 9-17:30, July, Aug 9-18 and evening tours (waterworks only) 19, 20, 21 and 22 o'clock. Folklore museum, ✆ 620808-500, Open: 1 April-31 Oct 10-17:30. Orangery, Open: Year-round, daily 9-16.

✖ **Pferdeschwemme**, built 1695 according to plans by Fischer von Erlach.

✖ **Glockenspiel**, Residenzplatz, ✆ 8042-2784. Open: Currently no tours due to renovations. Clockwork plays daily 7, 11, 18 o'clock (except during "Jedermann" performance. Changed times are posted on signs). The 35 bells were made in Antwerp. The clockwork was installed under Prince Bishop Johann Ernest Graf Thun in 1702.

✖ **Castle cable car**, Festungsgasse 4, ✆ 8884-9750, Open: Jan-April and 1 Oct- 31 Dec, 9-17, 1 May-31 Aug, 9-22, 1 Sept-30 Sept, 9-21. Departure every 10 minutes.

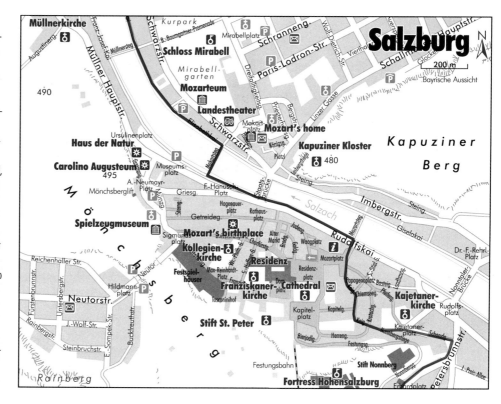

- ⬛ **Mönchsberg elevator**, Gstätteng. 13, ✆ 8884-9750, Open: 1 Jan-30 June and 15 Sept-31 Dec, 9-18, 1 July-14 Sept, 9-21, 24 Dec 9-17, departures as needed.
- ⬛ **Viewing terrace**. Superb views of Salzburg from the terraces of the Museum der moderne Mönchsberg.
- ⬛ **"Jedermann" performances**. Special performances of "Jedermann" by Hugo v. Hofmannsthal during the Salzburger Festspiele in the summer.
- ⬛ **Radio taxi with bicycle transport**, ✆ 8111 or ✆ 1715; Call in advance.
- ⬛ **Zoo Hellbrunn**, ✆ 820176, Open: Nov-Feb, daily 8:30-16, March, April daily 8:30-16:30 /17:30 during daylight saving time; May-mid Sept, 8:30-18:30, mid to late Sept, 8:30-17:30, Oct 8: 30-17. Gates close 16 o'clock after daylight saving time ends.

The city of Salzburg has a special magical quality – due at least in part to its status as the birthplace of Mozart – that the masses of tourists that flood the city only rarely see. Just the old city center, for instance, can be seen as a work of art. Watching the bustle in the narrow alleys and cobblestone streets from the window of an exquisitely decorated house in the city or on the slope of the Mönchsberg is bound to delight the soul, and convert the observer into a fan of the city that at one time was known to its friends as "the Rome north of the Alps."

Mirabell Palace

Salzburg's fame originated in the baroque period and has increased steadily since Mozart's day. In the 20th century the Salzburg Festival, which was first held in 1920, firmly established Salzburg's worldwide reputation.

The people of Salzburg today have a somewhat divided attitude about their city. On the one hand there is a strong desire to preserve traditions; on the other hand a well-developed business sense and the recognition of the inevitability of progress.

A visitor who makes the effort to look behind the commotion of the Festival and to explore the city when the tourists have left will discover "the real Salzburg." Browse in the lively market on the Mirabellplatz and the Universitätsplatz, enjoy the pale violet light that settles over the old city's houses in late afternoon, and savor the inviting smells of freshly-baked pastries and cake emanating from the cafés.

From Salzburg to Unzing   17 km

Go to the right bank of the Salzach and head north away from the old city center.

Tip: The Mozart Bike Trail follows the route of the Salzkammergut Bike Trail as it leaves Salzburg. Salzkammergut also offers excellent bicycle touring – many fine routes are described in the *bikeline* **Radatlas Salzkammergut (available in German)**.

Turn right away from the river a few meters before you go under the Autobahn bridge.

Tip: The Tauern Bike Trail follows the right bank of the Salzach. This tour is described in the *bikeline* **Radtourenbuch Tauern-Radweg (available in German)**.

The paved hiking/biking path follows the course of the Alterbach (stream) ～ proceed in the direction of the Gaisberg as far as the railroad underpass ～ and go through two tunnels under roads ～ and turn left onto the bicycle path along the main road ～ after 300 meters turn right on **Samstraße** ～ through an old tunnel under the railroad ⁓ follow the path past a post that blocks the way for regular traffic.

From this point the trail follows the right-of-way of the old Ischlerbahn, a narrow-gauge railroad that connected Salzburg and Bad Ischl from 1891 to 1957. The steam-powered train went out of service for economic reasons.

Continue straight through pastures and meadows ⁓ the Gaisberg looms above to the right ⁓ 400 meters past a cute chapel take the wooden bridge across a road ⁓ then cross a larger road ⁓ and ride through a pleasant little woods ⁓ at the turnoff for the villages of Zilling and Esch continue straight towards Eugendorf ⁓ and to the imposing long Autobahn bridge.

Stay on the Ischlerbahn path as it goes under the Autobahn ⁓ and runs next to the main road (Bundesstraße 1) ⁓ take the **Sofienweg** through the Sofien neighborhood ⁓ turn left on **Dürn-bichlerstraße** ⁓ and continue straight towards the church and the center of town.

Eugendorf

Postal code: A-5301; Telephone area code: 06225

🛈 **Tourism association**, Salzburger Str. 7, ✆ 8424, Fax 7773, www.eugendorf.com

5 St. Martin parish church, built 1736/37 on the site of a church first built in 788. The crucifixion ensemble is the work of the baroque sculptor Meinrad Guggenbichler.

The earliest recorded mention of Eugendorf dates from the year 736 during the rule of Duke Hubert von Bayern. During the middle ages many aristocratic families were drawn to the town, including the Kalhamers, a powerful family loyal to the archbishop. They owned extensive land holdings and performed many military duties, granted fiefs and established an order of knights. They were also responsible for Eugendorf's courts for more than 200 years.

In the late 20th century Eugendorf enjoyed strong economic growth as many companies moved their operations to the town. Located conveniently close to the Autobahn, Eugendorf today is considered the gateway to Salzburg. It also has extensive sports facilities, including two of Austria's most modern and beautiful golf courses. Horse riding, bicycling, tennis, squash and ninepins are popular as well. Local customs and cultural traditions are also prized: open air concerts and street theatre are held in the summer months, plus a number of festivals and culinary events. Winter festivities include an advent market and the traditional "Perchtenlauf" during

Eugendorf

which masked residents parade through the town to drive away demons.

After passing the church turn right at the war memorial ~ then take the second right towards Henndorf ~ and immediately turn into the field track, ignoring the sign indicating a "dead-end" ~ ride through the pedestrian tunnel (low clearance – watch your head!) ~ then turn right on **Santnerweg** and proceed to **Alten Wienerstraße** ~ turn right and ride through Eugenbach to the intersection of **Schamingstraße**.

The Mozart Bike Trail turns right on Schamingstraße and goes under the main road ~ follow the road through **Schaming** ~ after two kilometers arrive at the large farm near Unzing.

Tip: At this junction you must decide whether you wish to turn right for the side trip to St. Gilgen before returning and resuming the main route, or whether you wish to turn left and skip the visit to St. Gilgen. If you turn left, turn to page 26 to pick up the route description from Unzing to Köstendorf. If you choose to proceed to St. Gilgen, you may also consider continuing on the alternative route from the Mondsee to the Irrsee on the Salzkammergut Bike Trail. The description for this route begins on page 22.

Unzing to St. Gilgen   27 km

Turn right towards St. Gilgen to **Thalgauer Landesstraße** ~ turn left in **Kraiwiesen** ~ a bicycle/pedestrian path runs along the side of the main road to the inn in **Neuhofen** ~ the path goes under the road.

Continue 4 kilometers along the road ~ just before the Thalgau Autobahn access road turn right ~ ride 150 meters and turn left ~ and proceed straight along the Mitterbach (stream) to the sign bearing the name Unterdorf ~ take the main road for about 100 meters ~ the scenery

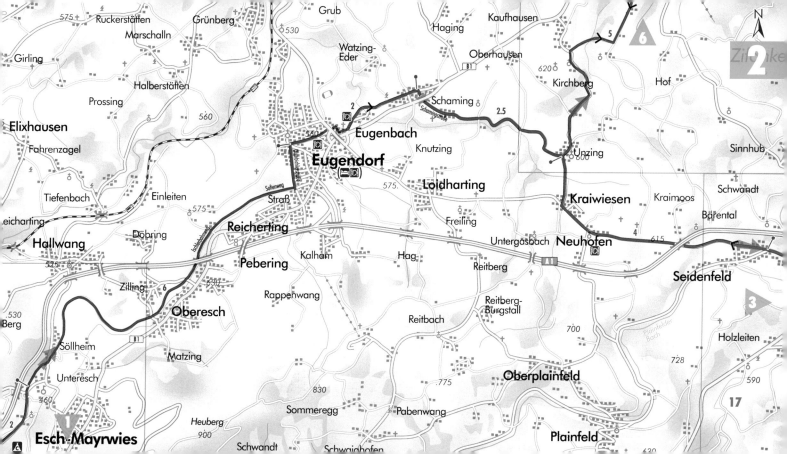

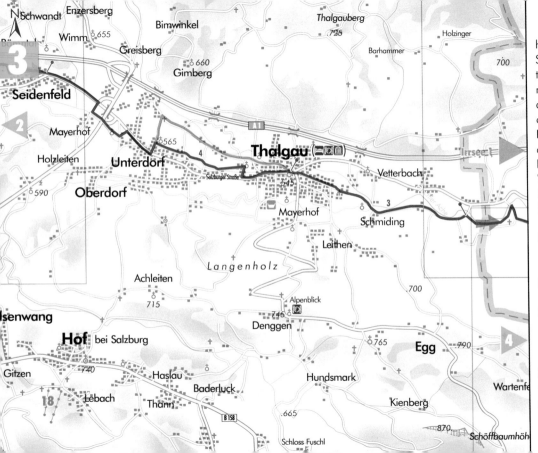

here is dominated by the stone formations of the Schober and the Drachenwand ∼ in **Unterdorf** turn left at the bus stop, cross the bridge and immediately turn right ∼ pass the fire department and continue along the Mitterbach in the direction of the Thalgau church tower ∼ pass **Gasthaus Betenmacher** and turn right at the sawmill and cross the bridge ∼ to **Salzburger Straße** ∼ turn left into the center of Thalgau.

Thalgau

Postal code: A-5303; Telephone area code: 06235

- *i* **Tourismusverband Thalgau**, Marktplatz 4, ☏ 7350, www.thalgau.at
- **Hundsmarktmühle**, Egg 24, ☏ 6417 or ☏ 6363, Open: July-Oct, Sat 14-17. Exhibits on the history of Thalgau and special exhibitions.
- **Dekanat Church**. Built 1745-55 by Tobias Kendler on the site of an early gothic church.
- **Burg Wartenfels**. The old walls built into the rocks at the foot of the Schober are the remains of a mountain keep and palace dating back to the 13th century.

The earlier recorded mention of Thalgau dates back to the year 788, when it was named as "Talgove" in one of the oldest surviving official documents of Salzburg. In 1259 Konrad von

Kahlham built a castle which he presented to the archbishop of Salzburg in 1301. The castle served as the home of a local court until it was moved to Thalgau in 1564, after which the unused castle fell into disrepair and deteriorated into the ruin that remains today. During the 30-years war Thalgau played an important role in the defense of the region, after archbishop Paris Lodron built an armory in the town. In 1976 the growing town gained the status of "Marktgemeinde." Today Thalau is known as "The Gateway to Salzkammergut" and has established itself as a favorite destination for tourism and recreation.

The route takes **Ferdinand Zuckerstätter Straße** towards Mondsee and St. Lorenz ~ at the market fountain stay to the right towards the schools complex ~ pass the schools and ride out of Thalgau ~ towards Vetterbach past the wastewater treatment plant ~ the bicycle trail winds along the **Fuschler Ache** (stream) through meadows along the foot of the Schober towards Kanten.

Tip: The stone marker stands on the border between the provinces of Salzburg and Oberösterreich. At this point the bicycle route signs also change from "Salzkammergut-Radweg" to "Mondseelandweg."

Turn right at the wayside shrine ~ after one kilometer turn right again towards the ruins of Burg Wartenfels and the Schober ~ turn left at the small traffic island with the three young birch trees ~ turn right on the main road ~ the route proceeds through fields and pastures dotted with farms and single-family homes ~ take the wooden bridge across the Fuschler Ache and arrive at the **Wagnermühle**.

Tip: The alternative route to Mondsee and Irrsee starts with a left turn at this junction.

Continue along the Fuschler Ache in the direction of the twin towers of the church in St. Lorenz.

Tip: There is an old linden tree in front of the renovated church, and an inviting inn from which one can take a rest and study the imposing Drachenwand cliff that rises over the Mondsee.

At the Plomberg town sign the route joins the **B 154** main national road ~ take the bicycle path to Scharfling ~ the Schafberg now dominates the view ~ follow the bicycle path through **Scharfling** ~ and continue about 2.5 kilometers along the **B 154** up to the Scharflinger heights.

Tip: As an alternative to the main road there is an idyllic path through meadows and woods that shortens the distance to St. Gilgen by 1.5 kilometers. This alternative is steep – tourists with baggage on their bicycles will probably need to dismount and push up some of the steepest sections. Even so, this alternative should be seriously considered, especially in the summer or on weekends when traffic on the main road is particularly heavy.

This unposted alternative route starts with a right turn just before you reach the Gasthof Scharlingerhof ~ after 200 meters at the fork go left on the gravel track and proceed straight ~ after about 300 meters the steep 1-kilometer-long climb begins ~ after the steepest part arrive at the B 154 main road just before the Scharflinger Höhe. (See the orange route on Map 5).

Descend gently from the **Scharflinger Höhe**.

Tip: The dark green Krottensee lies nestled

in the landscape below Schloss Hüttenstein. The Gasthof Batzenhäusl offers a pleasant place to enjoy the idyllic scenery.

After a long curve to the left, turn left where the bicycle route sign indicates the direction to St. Gilgen ~ take **Mondseer Straße** through a small woods and pass the handsome villas as you enter the center of the town.

St. Gilgen

Postal code: A-5340; Telephone area code: 06227

🛈 **Tourism association**, Mondsee Bundesstraße 1A, ☎ 2348, Fax 2348-9

⛴ **Wolfgangsee Schifffahrt und Schafbergbahn**, St. Wolfgang, Markt 35, ☎ 06138/2232-0, Open: May to Oct

🏛 **Musical instruments museum**, Aberseestr. 11, ☎ 06227/8235, Open 1 June-15 Oct, Tues-Sun 9-11 and 15-19. 16 Oct-6 Jan, Mon-Fri 9-11 and 14-17, 7 Jan-31 May, Mon-Thu 9-11 and 14-17, Fri 9-11, Sun 15-18. Museum with 1800 musical instruments and exhibits about music, customs and cultures of countries and tribes around the world.

🏛 **Local folklore museum**, Pichlerpl. 6, ☎ 2642, Open: June-Sept, Tues-Sun 10-12 and 14-18.

🏛 **Museum of Zinkenbacher painters**, Alberseestraße 11/1. Stock, ☎ 0676/7430916, Open: 15 June-15 Sept, Tues-Sun 15-19. Museum about a group of painters who worked together at the Wolfgangsee in the 1920s and 30s. www.malerkolonie.at

⛪ **St. Aegydius parish church**. This gothic church with a pointed steeple was built 1300 and was the site of numerous events in the Mozart family history, including his grandparent's marriage (1712), his mother's baptism (1720), his sister's marriage (1784), and the burials of his grandfather and brother-in-law.

⛪ **Schloss Hüttenstein**. Built in the romantic style in 1843 on the site of an old ruin

🚠 **Zwölferhorn cable car**, Raiffeisenpl. 3, ☎ 2350, daily 9-18. To 1522 meters elevation for hiking, paragliding, skiing.

✱ **Mozart monument**, Ischler Str. 15, Open:

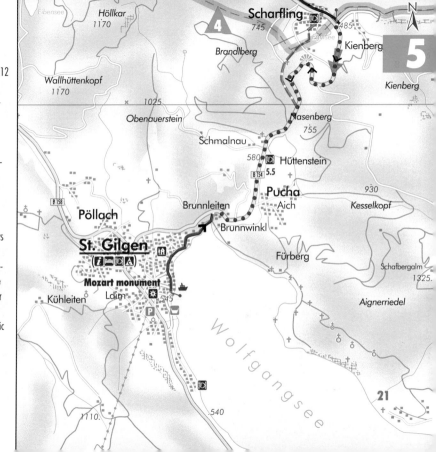

June to Sept, Tues-Sun 10-12 and 14-18. Anna Maria Walburga Pertl, Mozart's mother, was born December 25, 1720 in St. Gilgen. For 17 years this was also the home of Mozart's sister, Maria Anna Walburga Ignatia, after she married the man who succeeded her grandfather as local magistrate.

The former district court in **St. Gilgen**, which today houses the Mozart monument, was built as the "Pfleghaus" of Wolfgang Nikolaus Pertl, the grandfather of Wolfgang Amadeus Mozart. Pertl was a successful attorney and served as the magistrate in St. Gilgen.

Mozart's mother, Anna Maria Walburga Pertl, was born in the house on December 25, 1720 and baptized on the same day in the nearby St. Aegydius parish church. She spent the first four years of her life in the village.

By a stroke of fate or coincidence, W.A. Mozart's sister "Nannerl" on August 23, 1784 married the baron Johann Baptist Berchtold, the man who succeeded her grandfather as magistrate in St. Gilgen. She lived the next 17 years in what had been her mother's home and birthplace.

On the street side of the memorial is a relief by the sculptor Jakob Gruber, first unveiled in 1906, showing Mozart's mother and Nannerl.

St. Gilgen

In front of the building there is an inviting garden with a fountain by Toni Schneider Manzell. It shows Mozart's mother as a small girl. The Mozart fountain on St. Gilgen's Mozartplatz dates from 1927 and was created by the Viennese art-nouveau sculptor Prof. Karl Wollek.

From St. Gilgen to Unzing   27 km

Return by the same route as far as Wagnermühle.

Wagnermühle

Tip: The alternative route to the north via Mondsee and Irrsee diverges from the main route at Wagnermühle. Simply follow the Salzkammergut Bike Trail to Köstendorf. This route is very scenic as it skirts the Mondsee, passes through the charming village of the same name and proceeds via the Irrsee to Oberhofen and then Straßwalchen, two of the more noteworthy towns in the Salzkammergut.

Along the Irrsee   29 km

In Wagnermühle turn right towards Mondsee ~ cross the bridge and follow the Mondseeland Bike Trail sign ~ cross the **Fuschler Ache** (stream) and go to the main road ~ turn left for a short stretch ~ and then turn right immediately after the bus stop ~ onto the road to Mooshäusl.

Mooshäusl

After two curves to the left the road straightens out ~ go up hill and follow the road as it bends to the right ~ then turn right into the residential street ~ and proceed along the shore of the Mondsee through the village of Schwarzindien.

Schwarzindien

The unusual name Schwarzindien, which means "black India," dates to the beginning of the 20th century, when aristocratic families started coming to the Mondsee during the summer months. According to local lore, the youths from the area,

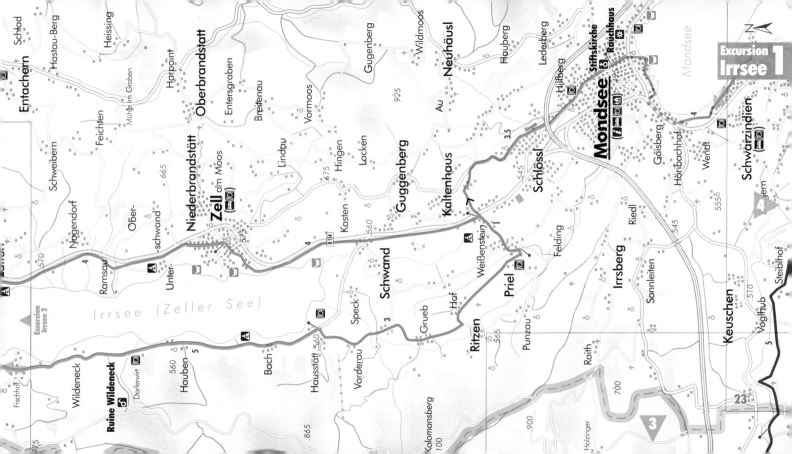

N

Entachern
Schlad
Hastau-Berg
Heissing
Schweibern
Feichten
Nagendorf
Ober-schwand
Ramsau
Unter-
Wildeneck
Fischhof
Ruine Wildeneck
Wildeneck
Dorferwirt
Hauben
Bach
Hausstätt
Vorderau
Speck
Grueb
Hof
Ritzen
Punzau
Raith
Holzinger
Kolomansberg

Harpoint
Mühle im Graben
Oberbrandstätt
Entersgraben
Entersau
Breitenau
Lindau
am Moos
Niederbrandstätt
Zell am Moos
Kasten
Hingen
Lacken
Vormoos
Vockla
Wildmoos
Gugenberg
Au

Schwand
Guggenberg
Kaltenhaus
Weißenstein
Priel
Felding
Sonnleiten
Irrsberg
Riedl
Keuschen
Voglhub
Steiblhof

Neuhäusl
Hauberg
Lederberg
Hilfberg
Stiftskirche
Mondsee
Rauchhaus
Mondsee
Hingen
Schlössl
Gaisberg
Höribachhof
Wendt
Schwarzindien

Irrsee (Zeller See)

Excursion
Irrsee 2

23

3

4

who also enjoyed the refreshing lake and spent their free time there, were driven away from the beaches to make the area more attractive to the wealthier visitors. This the local youths did not like, so they built themselves a raft and attempted to recapture their beach. As the darkly tanned youths approached the beach, the vacationing people yelled, "the black Indians coming." The youths liked this moniker, and drew up a flag which local authorities officially acknowledged. Since then the area has been called Schwarzindien.

At the end of the residential street ~ continue straight along the main street ~ and pass the Höribachhof.

Höribachhof

The renovated Höribachhof was originally the dairy for the Mondsee monastery and still looks as it did when it was built in the 15th century. Today it is used for exhibitions, concerts, seminars and meetings. It may also be rented for private functions like weddings and birthdays. For further information contact: ✆ 06232/27585.

Gaisberg comes next.

Gaisberg

The bicycle route turns to the right ~ and passes a sawmill ~ return to the street and then turn right ~ the town of Mondsee is one kilometer away ~ pass the **Gasthof Lackner on the right and proceed to** Mondsee Süd ~ cross the Zeller Ache ~ and pass the **Alpenseebad beach** ~ and turn left to the center of Mondsee.

Mondsee

Postal code: A-5310; Telephone area code: 06232

🛈 **Tourismusverband**, Dr.-Müller-Str. 3, ✆ 2270

⛴ **Mondsee Schifffahrt**, ✆ 4934, 2195, Open: April-Oct

🏛 **Rauchhaus (smokehouse)**, Freilichtmuseum, ✆ 2270, Open: after 18 April Sat, Sun, Hol 10-17; 1 May-7 Sept, Tues-Sun 10-18; 8 Sept-5 Oct, Tues-Sun 10-17; 6-26 Oct, Sat, Sun, Hol 10-17. An original old farmhouse with traditional furnishings.

🏛 **Heimat and Pfahlbau local history museum**, Schloss Mondsee, ✆ 2270, Open: 1 May-29 June, Tues-Sun 10-17; 30 June-7 Sept, Tues-Sun 10-18; 8 Sept-5 Oct, Tues-Sun 10-17; 6 Oct-26 Oct, Sat, Sun, Hol 10-17.

🏛 **Salzkammergut railroad museum**, Seebadstr. 2, ✆ 2270, Open: 7 June-14 Sept, Sat, Sun, Hol 10-12 and 14-17; 4 July-12 Sept also open Fri 14-17.

🏛 Former **Benedictine monastery**. The third-oldest monastery in Austria, from 748 to 1786. After a major fire in the monastery it was rebuilt 1774-78 as a palace. Today it is home to the local history museum.

🏛 **St. Michael monastery church**, the yellow basilica from 1470 has a magnificent baroque interior.

🏛 **Market square** surrounded by many noteworthy houses built in the 16th, 17th and 18th centuries.

Take **Herzog Odilo Straße** through the quaint old city center ~ and continue straight at the **Gasthof Grüner Baum** ~ after the Autobahn swing right on Güterweg Hingen ~ and proceed through **Schlössl** straight towards a recently-built residential area ~ and follow the Mondseelandweg signs to the left down to the B 154 main road.

Tip: At the B 154 you have the option of taking an alternative route to Zell am Moos and along the eastern shore of the Irrsee to Laiten. At the north end of the lake you can rejoin the route to Oberhofen. This alternative route mostly runs along the main road. Zell am Moos is worth a visit – the eastern shore is said to be especially beautiful in the twilight hours of evening.

Zell am Moos

Postal code: A-4893; Telephone area code: 06234

🛈 **Tourism association Zell am Moos**, Kirchenplatz 1, ✆ 8215, Fax 82154, www.zellammoos.at

🏛 **Irrseer Heimathaus**, Dorfstr. 20, ☎ 7025. Folklore collection of Hans Mayrhofer-Irrsee, with Irrsee pottery, garden gallery and art studio.

⛪ **Kolomann church.** Austria's oldest wooden church is located on the Kolomannsberg high above the Irrsee.

To stay on the main route cross the road at the warehouse at **Weißenstein** and ride to **Haidermühle** ~ make a sharp right turn here ~ and after about one kilometer follow the sign for Oberhofen at the fork in the road.

Arrive at the **Hotel Pöllmann** at the western shore of the Irrsee ~ follow the small hilly country road as it proceeds above the lake to the north end of the Irrsee ~ pass numerous pleasant looking inns, campgrounds and large farms ~ turn left before you reach the B 154 near the village of Laiten ~ turn right 800 meters later ~ proceed a few meters and then veer left on the narrow field path ~ which leads towards the church in Oberhofen in the distance ~ at the edge of town the route curves to the left towards the center of Oberhofen.

Oberhofen am Irrsee
Postal code: A-4894; Telephone area code: 06213

ℹ **Tourism association**, No. 12, ☎ 8273, Fax 2154

⛪ **Parish church with** Guggenbichler altars.

Boats on Mondsee

🏰 **Wildeneck ruin.** Earthen walls and wall remnants are all that remain of the once-important 13th century castle and court.

Starting in Oberhofen, the route is once again indicated by signs for the Salzkammergut Radweg ~ proceed straight at the **Oberhofen-Zell am Moos train station** ~ after the underpass under the tracks continue straight to the B 154 ~ turn left and go about 700 meters ~ pass a stone marking the border of Salzburg province ~ and turn left towards Taigen ~ turn right after 300 meters ~ and ride through the lush meadows to reach **Irrsdorf** ~ notice the unusual wooden hut used by the carrier pigeon club ~ and follow the course of the stream through Irrsdorf.

Cross to the other side of the street and pass the recently-built row-houses in the Thalham neighborhood ~ in Thalham pass the **Gasthof Asen** and a unique building that reflects an architect's creative fantasies ~ the bicycle route runs along the left side of the B 154 to the junction with the Bundesstraße 1 ~ the Salzkammergut bicycle route crosses this Bundesstraße and proceeds on **Köstendorfer Straße** ~ the center of Strasswalchen is to the right.

Strasswalchen
Postal code: A-5204; Telephone area code: 06215

ℹ **Tourism association**, Salzburger Str. 26., ☎ 6420, Fax 5455

⛪ **St. Martin parish church.** 15th century church was redone in the baroque style in the 18th century. The main altar from 1675 is the first significant work done by Meinrad Guggenbichler.

✖ **Straßwalchen amusement park**, north of Straßwalchen on the B 1, ☎ 8181, Open: May to Oct, 10-18. Games and fun for the whole family.

✖ **Balloon rides**; contact the tourism office for information about hot air balloon rides.

〰 **Swimming center**, ☎ 6420, Open: daily 10-19.

The name Strasswalchen is probably derived from the word "walchen" – the name that invading Bavarian tribes gave to the romanized **25**

Celts and remaining Romans they found in the region. The earliest recorded mention of Strasswalchen dates to 799, but archaeological finds in the area suggest it was probably settled at least 2000 years BC. In 1458 it was granted market rights by Archbishop Burkhard II von Weisspriach. Over the following centuries the town suffered several major fires and was plundered by French armies. Strasswalchen started to thrive only after the arrival of the railroad. Today it is a prosperous town that many city dwellers continue to move to for its quiet country charm.

Ride through a cluster of townhouses on **Köstendorfer Straße** ～ cross the tracks and follow the small country lane towards Köstendorf.

Köstendorf
Postal code: A-5203; Telephone area code: 06216

🛈 **Town offices**, Kirchenstr. 5, ✆ 5313

🏛 **Local history museum**, ✆ 6554, Open: June-Sept, Sat 9-12 or by appointment. Contains information about the history of Köstendorf, the painter Joseph Mösl, handicrafts, traditional dress, hunting, farm equipment and local folklore.

🛐 **Dekanat parish church**, built in the 15th century. Was an important pilgrimage church until the 18th century.

Strasswalchen

The area around Köstendorf was already settled between 1200 and 500 BC. The earliest known reference to Köstendorf dates to 788 AD. One of its best known native sons is the portrait painter Joseph Mösl, who was born January 13, 1821 in the Moosmühle. He was initially trained as a miller, before being "discovered" by Archbishop Friedrich VI of Salzburg. He studied under the painter Sebastian Stief and attended the Munich Art Academy from 1842 to 1846. In the following years he helped paint the interior of the Speyer cathedral and produced most of his body of work. He died in 1851 in the house of his birth. Many of his works can be seen in Salzburg's Museum Carolino Augusteum. In Köstendorf he is honored with a marble plaque on the wall of the cemetery.

Tip: In Köstendorf the alternative route via Mondsee and Irrsee rejoins the main route of the Mozart Bike Trail which came from Henndorf to the south.

Unzing to Köstendorf   18 km
To stay on the main route, turn left in Unzing, away from the Salzkammer Radweg (map 6).
Unzing
Ride past the church and turn left at the edge of the village ～ on **Unzingstraße** follow the bike sign towards Henndorf ～ make the right-hand loop through one farm ～ and then gently uphill in another right-handed curve past the next farm ～ and take **Kirchbergstraße** into the woods ～ the Kirchberg with its small church can be seen to the left ～ then back downhill through the hamlet ～ follow the bicycle sign to the right at the electricity transformer station ～ downhill over a wooden bridge and then back uphill ～ turn left at the next junction ～ and take **Schönbergstraße** towards Henndorf ～ after a curve to the right cross the

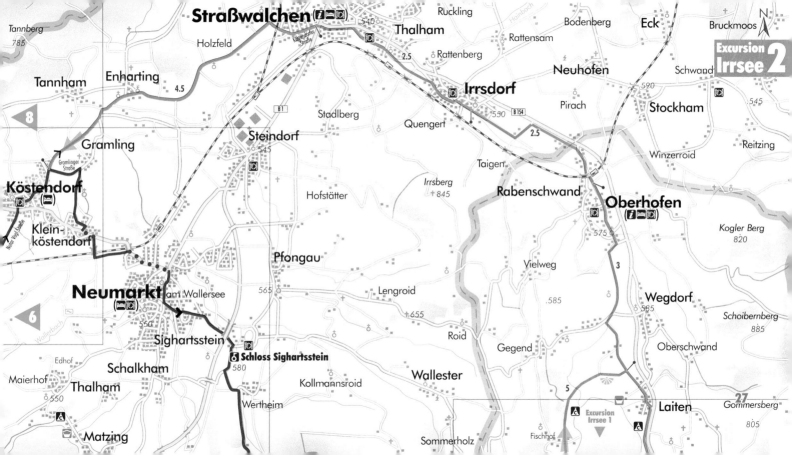

N

Straßwalchen (i) 🏛️ 🏛️

Tannberg
785

Ruckling

Bodenberg

Eck

Bruckmoos

Holzfeld

540

Thalham

Rattensam

Schwand

Enharting

2.5

Rattenberg

Neuhofen

590

Tannham

4.5

Stadlberg

Quengert

Irrsdorf

Pirach

Stockham

545

B1

550

B 154

Reitzing

Steindorf

2.5

Winzerroid

Gramling

545

Irrsberg
+ 845

Taigen

Rabenschwand

Gramlinger Straße

Hofstätter

Oberhofen (i) 🏛️ 🏛️

Kogler Berg
820

Köstendorf 🏛️ 🛏️

575

Klein-
köstendorf

Vielweg

3

Wegdorf
585

Nöfa Vogl Straße

Pfongau

585

Oberschwand

Schoibernberg
885

Neumarkt am Wallersee 🛏️🏛️

565

Lengroid

+ 655

Roid

550

Sighartsstein

🔔 **Schloss Sighartsstein**
580

Gegend

5

Laiten

Gommersberg
805

Edhof

Schalkham

Kollmannsroid

Wallester

🏕️ **Excursion Irrsee 1** ▼

Maierhof

Thalham
550

Wertheim

Sommerholz

Fischhof

🏕️

6

8

7

27

intersecting road ~ and ride past pastures to a small wooden bridge ~ turn left at the following T-intersection and head into Henndorf.

Henndorf

Postal code: A-5302; Telephone area code: 06214

🛈 **Tourism association**, Hauptstr. 65, ✆ 6011

✉ Beach and outdoor pool, ✆ 8263

🏨 **Gasthof Caspar Moser Bräu**, ✆ 8228. One of the oldest inns in Austria, it was once a favorite haunt of Carl Zuckmayer and many other artists. Today the traditional "Carl Zuckmayer Jause" is still served.

✿ **Eiszeitrundweg (Ice age trail)** – informative hiking trail.

Follow **Alte Tannstraße** ~ and turn right on **Bergstraße** and follow the signs for the **Zuckmayer** route towards **Neumarkt** ~ stay on Bergstraße through the hilly countryside ~ and turn left when you reach the larger road ~ ride downhill, then back uphill ~ the village of Berg is to the right ~ stay right when you reach the next right-of-way road ~ gently downhill and to the left across a bridge ~ stay left on the flat paved road ~ and follow the road as it skirts the edge of the forest ~ go straight at the intersection ~ and take the unpaved road to Haslach.

Haslach

In the village stay left at the intersection ~ and

continue along the Zuckmayer Route on a paved road ~ the Steinbach stream is to the right, a forest to the left ~ and soon you enter Wertheim.

Wertheim

Turn left at the intersection ~ and turn right at the sign at the edge of the village ~ **Sighartstein** comes next ~ turn left at the **Schlossgastwirtschaft** and proceed under the road towards Neumarkt.

Neumarkt am Wallersee

Postal code: A-5202; Telephone area code: 06216

🛈 **Tourism office**, Hauptstr. 30, ✆ 6907

🏛 **Museum in der Fronfeste**, Hauptstr. 27, ✆ 5704, Open: May-Oct, Tues, Thurs, Sat and Sun 14-17. Exhibits about the courts system, the Romans, hatmaking, leather working and tanning, and various special exhibitions.

On December 23 one year, Mozart and his family spent the night in Neumarkt before proceeding to Roverto the next day. Today Neumarkt holds a traditional autumn farm festival in September to celebrate the successful harvest. Events include farmers market and the preparation of traditional foods made from local produce, to insights into local farming traditions and customs as well as the opportunity to sample specialties like "Bauerngeselchtes," "Vogelbeerschnaps" or "Knoflkas".

Proceed downhill and across a small bridge ~ uphill at the main road ~ turn right and through the center of the town ~ turn left on Bahnhofstraße following the sign towards Köstendorf ~ and turn left on the narrow path just before the bridge over the railroad tracks ~ and ride out of Neumarkt ~ ride parallel to the railroad for 500 meters and then turn right over a bridge across the tracks ~ go straight and then turn left on the main road.

Kleinköstendorf

After a few meters turn right towards Johannesberg ~ ride around the Johannesberg and then turn left on **Gramlingerstraße** ~ and turn left again on **Enhartingerstraße** ~ and then onto **Untere Dorfstraße** and then left uphill over the **Wirtsberg**.

Köstendorf

Köstendorf to Mattsee   14 km

Cross the main road ~ and go straight on **Notar Vogl Straße** ~ under the high-tension wires and downhill ~ the road curves to the right as it approaches the railroad line and then follows the tracks ~ go straight ahead where the bridge crosses the tracks ~ the Eisbach stream is to the left ~ the road curves to the right around a

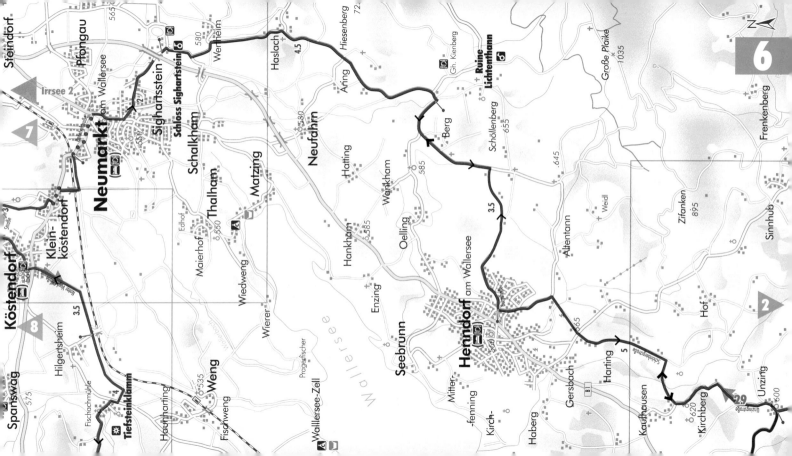

Tannberg
Holzfeld
Tannham
Enharting
4.5
Gramling
Steindorf
Köstendorf
Johannesberg
3
Klein-köstendorf
560
3.5
Neumarkt am Wallersee
545
565
550
Sighartsstein
2
Edhof
Schloss Sighartsstein
Schalkham
Maierhof
580
550
Thalhäm
Wertheim
Wiedweng
Matzing
Wierer

sawmill ~ turn right on the main road and then immediately left again.

Fischachmühle

Go uphill into the woods ~ stay left at the fork.

Tip: The Tiefsteinklamm is 100 meters further to the left.

Behind the forest the steeple of the church in Schleedorf is visible.

Schleedorf

Postal code: A-5205; Telephone area code: 06216

🛈 **Tourism association**, Dorf 95, ☎ 6911
🛈 **Town offices Schleedorf**, Dorf 104, ☎ 4100
🏛 **Agri-Cultur museum**, Schleedorf Dorf 95, ☎ 6911, Fax DW 4.
Prize-winning museum with exhibits about nature and agriculture built around the collections of one of Salzburg's most important nature researchers, with butterfly collections, a living bee colony as well as flora and fauna. Temporary exhibitions.

✳ **Schleedorfer Puppet window.** Under the title "the clothes make the person," an artistic display featuring 60 puppets that give an entertaining account of how clothes developed. Admission tickets can be obtained from the Agri-Cultur museum to see the puppets in motion with musical accompaniment.

✳ **Spieleweg (games path).** For families with children, a walking path with 10 stations where simple but clever games can be played. Shows how the games children play have changed in recent years.

✳ **Salzburger Käsewelt**, Moos 1, ☎ 4198, Fax DW 4, www.kaesewelt.at. Open: Mon-Sat 8-17, Sun 10-17. Make your own cheese: Tues, Thurs and Sat at 10:30 to 12:30. Guided tours and film: daily at 10, 12 and 14 if at least five adults present. Experience the world of cheese, how milk is made into cheese. Churn your own butter: Weds 14 o'clock. There is also a restaurant with various kinds of cheese specialties.

Ride past the playing field and follow the roadway ~ past the church ~ and turn left ~ pass the stalls and then turn left towards Käsewelt ~ after the supermarket turn left towards Engerreich/Mattsee ~ this path is marked with signs "Salz und Seen Tour" ~ at the last house turn right onto the small road with the sign limited to vehicles

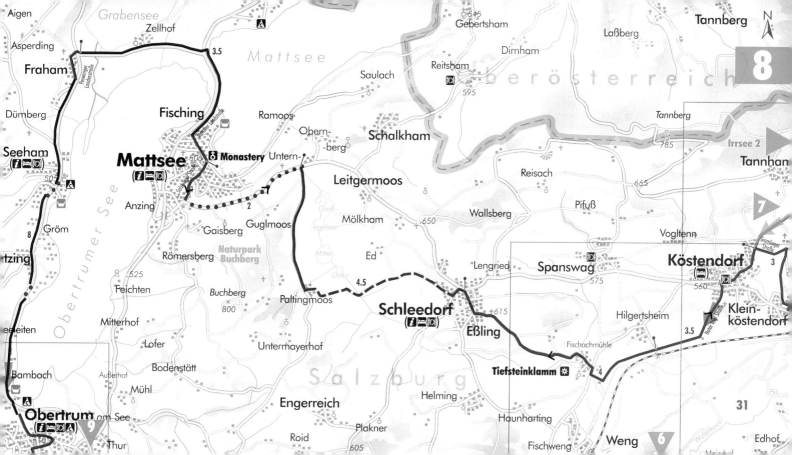

Aigen
Grabensee
Zellhof
545
Gebertsham
Laßberg
Tannberg

N

Asperding
Fraham
Mattsee
Dirnham
berösterreich

Dümberg
Fisching
Ramoos
Saulach
Reitsham
595
Tannberg
785
Irrsee 2

Seeham
Obern-berg
Schalkham
Tannhan

50
Mattsee
Monastery
Untern-
Leitgermoos
Reisach
665
7

Anzing
2
Pifuß
Wallsberg

8
Gröm
Gaisberg
Guglmoos
Mölkham
650
Spanswag
575
Vogltenn
Köstendorf
3

tzing
Römersberg
Naturpark Buchberg
Mitter
Ed
Lengried
Hilgertsheim
560
Klein-köstendorf

Feichten
525
Buchberg 800
Unter
4.5
Paltingmoos
615
Schleedorf
Eßling
Fischachmühle
3.5

eeleiten
Mitterhof
Untermayerhof
Salzburg
Tiefsteinklamm
4

Bambach
Außerhof
Lofer
Bodenstätt
Mühl
Helming
Haunharting
31

Obertrum am See
9
Thur
Engerreich
Roid
Plakner
605
Fischweng
Weng
6
Edhof

under 8 tons ～ stay left at the edge of town and follow the track through the meadows ～ the asphalt on the track comes to an end ～ proceed a short stretch along the edge of a forest ～ take the right turn-left turn combination around a farm.

Paltingmoos

At the intersection turn right. The road is paved ～ ride past the Unteregelsee and Mitteregelsee lakes towards Guglmoos.

Guglmoos

Ride past the Großegelsee ～ and follow the left curve down to the main road ～ where you turn left ～ the right shoulder is wide and enables cyclists to stay out of traffic ～ the road offers excellent views to the right as it descends down to Mattsee ～ ride into the town ～ following bicycle route signs for the right turn into **Salzburger Straße** ～ and bear left around the church.

Mattsee

Postal code: A-5163; Telephone area code: 06217

🔰 Tourism association Mattsee, ✆ 6080

🏛 Monastery museum, ✆ 5202-30, Open: June-Aug, Thurs and Sat 17-19, Sun 11-12; Sept and Octn Sun 11-12. Museum about the history, art and treasures of the monastery. Exhibits include old documents, a library, religious art.

Bicyclists at Obertrum Lake

✳ **Bajuwaren Freilichtschau**, Weyerbucht, Open: June, Aug, daily 14-17, May-Sept, Sat,Sun,Hol 14-17, Oct, Sun,Hol 14-17.

🔖 **St. Michael monastery**. Benedictine abbey founded by Tassilo von Bayern and built 740-50. Expanded in the baroque style in 1765. The tower was added at this time.

⛺ **Naturpark Buchberg**

✉ **Beach**, ✆ 5252, Open: May-Sept, daily 8-19. Water slides, baby basin, beach volley ball, gymnastics, activities for children, Qi Gong.

🔧 **Firma Grabner**, Salzburger Str. 29, ✆ 6333. Also rents bicycles.

The earliest settlements in the area around Mattsee date to the late Stone Age. The monastery was established in 770 by Duke Tassilo III of Bavaria and gained further significance as a collegiate abbey in the 11th century. The first beach cabins were erected in 1869, as the town became increasingly popular as a tourism and vacation destination. The Wallmansbad was built one year later, bringing the first summer holidaymakers to Mattsee. The Moorbad was opened in 1903, followed by the public beach facilities in 1928. In 1935 Mattsee gained municipality status. Today it is still a popular summer recreation destination. It also has a special autumn attraction – the farmers harvest festival from late August through late October. Celebrations start with a car-free day on which food and beverages are offered throughout the center of town. Other attractions include the fisherman's festival with displays of prize fish, live fish and fishing equipment as well as the "three-lakes" folkdance organized by folkdance groups from Mattsee, Obertrum and Seeham.

Mattsee to Anthering   22.5 km

Take **Passauer Straße** to **Mattseer Landesstraße** ⁓ and ride along the bicycle path for 2 kilometers towards the north ⁓ at the major intersection follow signs to the left towards Seeham ⁓ after crossing two small wooden bridges the path reaches **Perwanger Landesstraße** ⁓ after crossing the main road continue straight into Fraham ⁓ ride right through a farmyard ⁓ and through Fraham above the main road ⁓ and return to the main road, which has a bicycle path running next to it.

The bicycle path ends at the intersection with **Obertrumer Landesstraße** ⁓ ride about 1 kilometer on busy streets through **Seeham** ⁓ the bicycle path starts again ⁓ and ends in Matzing ⁓ a bicycle lane starts in Bambach ⁓ turn right on **Seestraße** as you enter **Obertrum** ⁓ take Hauptstraße to reach the central square.

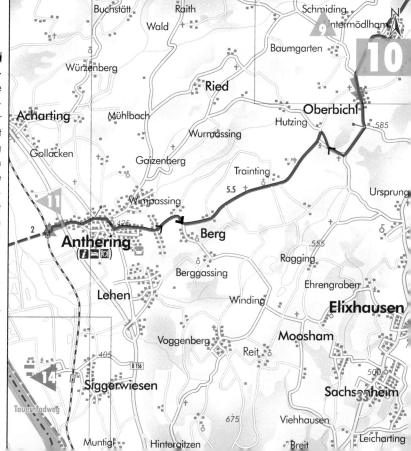

Obertrum

Postal code: A-5162; Telephone area code: 06219

- 🛈 **Tourismusverband**, Mattigplatz 1, ☎ 6307 or 6080
- 🏛 **Museum im Einlegerhaus**, Kirchstättstr. 23, ☎ 6582, Open: June-Aug, Tues 17-19 or by appointment. Farm pottery, flax production, food smoking and other topics.
- 🏛 **Puppenwelt**, Jakobistr. 6, ☎ 6307 or ☎ 6429, Open: Fri, Sat 14-18 or by appointment. Porcelain puppets, arts and crafts.
- ❊ **Historic Kaiser's beech on the** Haunsberg. A red beech planted in honor of the visit by Kaiser Josef II in 1779.

A brewery famous for its Trumer beer is located right next to the church.

Follow bicycle signs towards Anthering-Mödlham ~ turn right after the brewery restaurant (**Braugasthof**) ~ proceed 200 meters and turn left on **Mattichstraße** ~ and continue straight ahead through the hilly Flachgau countryside ~ the scenery is dotted with large farmsteads standing by themselves and pretty chapels along the sides of the roads.

Stay left in **Hamberg** ~ the route to Mödlham offers excellent views of the mountain scenery around Salzburg ~ the many single-family homes in **Untermödlham** reflect the growing popularity of vacation homes ~ stay left at the main road ~ and ride through the village of **Mödlham** ~ turn right at the house at the edge of the village ~ and right again at the cute shelter at the bus station ~ in **Hutzing** turn left where the bicycle sign is affixed to a barn ~ after **Trainting** a beautiful view into the Salzach valley opens up to the west ~ and the route goes down a steep hill towards the town of Anthering ~ and runs into a main road across from the town offices ~ turn right towards the main square.

Anthering

Postal code: A-5102; Telephone area code: 06223

- 🛈 **Tourism association**, Dorfstr. 1, ☎ 2279
- 🌿 **Herbal garden**, ☎ 2210 or ☎ 2350. Herbal garden with about 350 herbs, as well as a farmer's garden, wetlands, raised beds, a "garden of beauty," a "garden of scents," a "garden of rarities" and a "garden of poisons." Regular lectures, seminars and workshops covering the many uses of plants and herbs.
- 🏊 **Outdoor pool**, ☎ 2929, Open: daily 9-20.

The town of Anthering was established in the 6th century. It is best known for the legendary "Maunz devil," a fantastic beast that residents of the town are said to have seen on the nearby Haunsberg in the year 1532. The Maunzteufel had hoofed feet, a lion's tail, horse's mane and a human face topped

Trail near Anthering

with a cockscomb. Townspeople captured the beast in a ditch and it soon died because if refused all food. The stone statue in the center of town is supposed to testify to the existence of this creature. Today it's suspected the legend probably based on a severely deformed human who lived in the woods after being outcast because of his handicaps.

Anthering to Laufen   10 km

Before coming to the church, turn left on **Bahnhofsstraße** ~ after the tunnel under the main Bundesstraße the route leads to the **Anthering train station** ~ take an unpaved track under the railroad and head straight into the Salzach's flood plains and down to the river

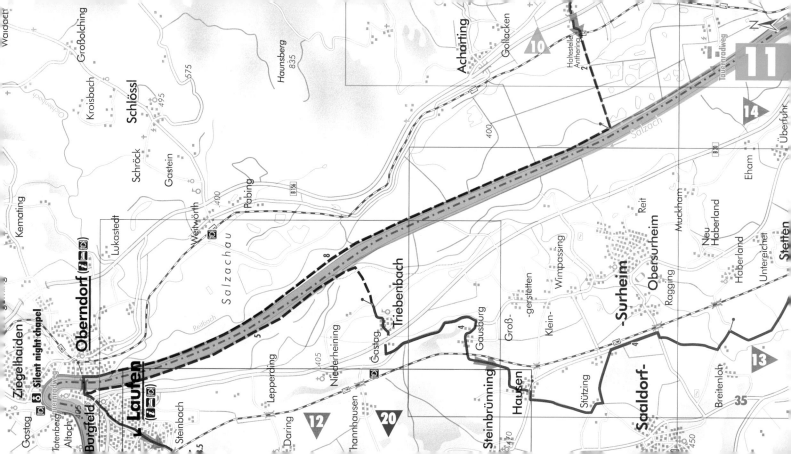

~ where the route meets the Tauernradweg ~ which runs along the right bank of the Salzach to Oberndorf.

Tip: In Oberndorf the Mozart Bike Trail turns to the west while the Tauernradweg continues along the bank of the Salzach River.

Oberndorf

Postal code: A-5110; Telephone area code: 06272

🛈 **Tourism association**, Stille-Nacht-Pl. 2, ✆ 4422

🏛 **"Bruckmannhaus" local history museum**, Stille-Nacht-Pl. 7, ✆ 7569, Open: daily 9-12 and 13-17. Exhibits about the Christmas carol "Silent Night, Holy Night," shipping on the Salzach, and town history.

🏛 **Shipping museum**, Salzburger Str. 88, ✆ 7569, Open: Guided tours by appointment. Numerous exhibits about shipping on the Salzach.

🔵 **Stille Nacht Kapelle**, chapel consecrated in 1937 on the site of the Nikola church, where the Christmas carol "Silent night, Holy night" was performed for the first time in 1818.

🔵 **Maria Bühel pilgrim church**, built 1670. Interior includes works my the imperial painter J. M. Rottmayr dating from late baroque to early rococo.

✳ **Boat rides** on the **Salzach**, ✆ 4422, Open: 23 May - 26 Sept, Sat, departure from Muntigl: 14 o'clock. Rides on original "Zillen" river boats from Muntigl near Salzburg (see map 14) to

Oberndorf. Muntigl can be reached from Salzburg or Oberndorf on an antique train.

Oberndorf is the town where the world-famous Christmas carol "Silent Night, Holy Night" was written by Joseph Mohr and Franz Xaver Gruber, who had the inspiration of writing "something special for the Holy night" in 1818. Mohr wrote the text and passed it to his friend Gruber, who set it to music for two soloists and a choir with guitar accompaniment. Gruber waited until the last minute, writing the music in the morning of December 24. Even in German-speaking countries, the carol did not become well-known until it was popularized in the United States.

Ride the riverside path to Oberndorf as far as the Salzach bridge ~ turn left to cross the river and the German-Austrian border and enter the town of Laufen.

Silent Night chapel

Laufen an der Salzach

Postal code: D-83410; Telephone area code: 08682

🛈 **Tourism association Abtsdorfer See**, Im Schlossrondell 2, ✆ 1810

🔵 **Mariä Ascension monastery**, gothic building finished in 1338, loggia with red marble memorial slabs.

🔵 **Archbishops palace**, erected 1608 by the Italian builder Vicenzo Scmozzi.

✳ **City square** with late-gothic city hall

After a three-and-a-half year tour to Paris and London, the Mozarts departed Munich on November 27, 1766 and passed through Altgötting and Laufen on their return to Salzburg. This trip represented a big investment for Leopold Mozart, though he was able to earn a profit by selling in Salzburg all the presents he and his son had collected during their trip.

Turn left at the intersection to head out of Laufen ~ ride through the town gate toward the next intersection.

From Laufen to Reit im Winkel

90.5 km

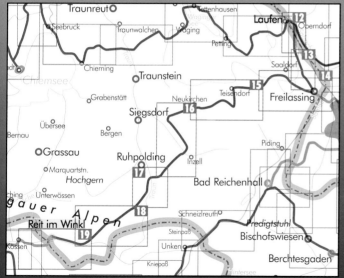

The second part of the tour leads from Laufen through the picturesque Kaiserwinkel region. The first highlight is the Bavarian border town of Freilassing, followed by densely forested slopes along the foothills of the Alps. A number of points along the route offer spectacular panoramas of the mountainous geography. The pretty route passes through the idyllic valley, around mountain lakes and cool, shady woods before reaching the popular tourist destination of Reit im Winkl.

Most of the route follows unpaved bicycle paths and farm/forest service roads. Significant traffic is present only in Reit. There are climbs between Teisendorf and Hammer.

Laufen

Laufen to Freilassing   16.5 km

Starting from **Marienplatz** swing into **Rott-mayr Straße** ~ and cross the **Stadtbrücke** and proceed a short piece on **Guckhaus Straße** ~ and onto the dike along the **Salzach** ~ under the bridge and along the river as far as the mouth of the Sur tributary ~ along the Sur dike to the Sursteg bridge ~ and then further upstream to Triebenbach.

Triebenbach

Ride through the village to the tunnel under the B 20 main road ~ through the tunnel and to Hauptstraße towards Surheim ~ turn right after 1.4 kilometers through **Gausburg towards** Hausen.

Hausen

From Hausen continue to **Stützing**, then turn left towards Surheim ~ and ride along the railroad ~ towards Freilassing-Brodhausen ~ after the man-made pond turn left through the tunnel under the railroad and onto **Bre-slauer Straße**, **Siebenbürger Straße** and **Obere Feldstraße** to where it meets **Münch-**

Laufen

ner Straße** and continue into the center of Freilassing.

Freilassing

Freilassing to Teisendorf   15 km

Ride out of town on **Münchner Straße, Was-serburger Straße** until you reach the Freilas-singer Freibad (outdoor pool) ~ and turn left towards Sillersdorf and then on to Patting.

Patting

Turn left towards Patting just before you reach Hauptstraße and ride past the "Tiefen-taler Hof" inn ~ at first the path goes through the Tiefenthaler forest before crossing meadows to Hörafing.

Hörafing

Ride through the village and through the tunnel under the B 304 main road ~ ride through **Kumpfmühle** and then right to Roßdorf ~ from **Roßdorf** take the BGL 10 road towards Teisendorf ~ before you reach the B 304 main road turn left onto the pedestrian/biking path that runs along the left side of the road ~ turn right under the B 304 and continue on towards **Grubenhaus** and **Wörlach** ~ ride past the tennis courts ~ and take **Roßdorfer Straße** down to **Alte Reichenhaller Straße** to **Markstraße** into the center of Teisendorfs.

Teisendorf

Postal code: D-83317; Telephone area code: 08666

🛈 Tourism office, Poststr. 14, ✆ 295

🏛 Bergbaumuseum Achthal, ✆ 7149 or ✆ 1029, Open: May-Sept, Tues, Thurs, Sun 10-12, Tues-Sat 13-16 or by appt. The mining museum is located in an old ore mine in the Teisenberg. It ceased production in 1925. Visitors can

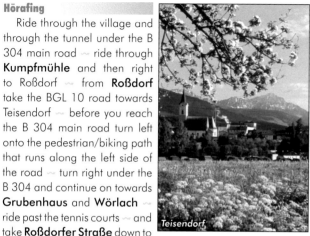
Teisendorf

learn about the work of miners, molders and casters.

⛰ Geological garden, ✆ 295

🚲 Berger, Poststr. 24, ✆ 6598

The earliest recorded mention of this roughly 1200-year old market dates to the year 790. Teisendorf acquired market rights in 1275. When the French invaded in 1800, Teisendorf surrendered without a fight to prevent the town's destruction. It surrendered in 1945 also. Today the town of Teisendorf has six districts and about 9,000 inhabitants. It benefits especially from the newly-configured historic Marktstraße, the M. C. Wieninger brewery and the Kolping Hotel.

Teisendorf to Inzell   24.5 km

Take **Marktstraße** to the left turn towards Freidling ~ ride past the furniture store on the right and continue on to Freidling.

Freidling

Turn right at the intersection towards Achthal and follow the main road to the intersection ~ turn left towards Allerberg ~ ride uphill over **Allerberg**, **Haslach** and **Fuchssteig** ~ stay on the main road through **Atzlbach** and **Loch** towards **Neukirchen** ~ turn left at the filling station and after about 150 meters ride under the Autobahn ~ follow the main road through Weitwies towards Siegsdorf.

After 2 kilometer come to the start of a bicycle path along the side of the road ~ which you follow to the St. Johann neighborhood.

St. Johann

Wolfgang Amadeus Mozart began his second trip to Italy on August 13, 1771, and spent the first night in St. Johann. He slept here a second time on October 24, 1772 during his third Italy trip.

Turn left towards Heutau ~ ride past the **St. Johann mill** and Gasthaus Heutau to the saw-mill ~ where you cross the bridge and then turn right on **Soleleitungsweg** to Hammer.

Hammer

In Hammer ride past the church and over a bridge ~ and over a second bridge ~ after the

Inzell

third small bridge turn right on **Hirschklause** and proceed towards Meisau ~ follow the road to Inzell ~ after **Kaßmühle** there is a wooden bridge ~ but the route turns left just before the bridge, towards Inzell ~ on to **Salinenweg** which is flat as it runs through the wide valley alongside a stream and past an inn.

Inzell

Postal code: D-83334; Telephone area code: 08665

🛈 **Inzeller Touristik GmbH**, Rathausplatz 5, ✆ 9885-0, Fax 988530, www.inzell.de (for accommodations and information)

🔲 **Einsiedl church St. Nikolaus**, can be reached by foot at the Einsiedlhof (45-minute walk). It is the oldest church in Inzell. Noteworthy are the St. Nikolaus figures and the three reliefs — the most significant of which is a depiction of a tree of life dating from about 1400.

🔲🔲 **Badepark (baths park) Inzell** with outdoor and indoor pools plus a Mediterranean sauna, ✆ 1633.

🔲 House in which **Anton Cajetan Adlgasser** was born, musician and friend of the Mozart family. Gasthof Neimoar, Schmelzer Str. 40.

🔲 **Zwingsee lake**, Eisstadion. Boat rental from Gerhard Dießbacher ✆ 300 and 1382.

🔲 **Inzell spa with herbal gardens and ponds**, is one of the most beautiful spas of its kind. Summer program includes concerts and traditional park festivals.

🔲 **Inzeller Eisstadion (ice skating stadium)**, well-known venue for national and international competitions and performances. The 400-meter artificial ice oval is a popular training and racing site for speed skaters from around the world.

🔲 Bicycle service and rental **Fahrrad Kötzinger**, Reichenhaller Str. 21, ✆ 310.

Inzell was the hometown of Anton Cajetan Adlgasser, who is probably the most famous musician to come out of the Chiemgau region of southern Bavaria. He was born in Inzell's schoolhouse (today the "Beim Neimoar" inn) on October 1, 1729 and died December 21, 1777

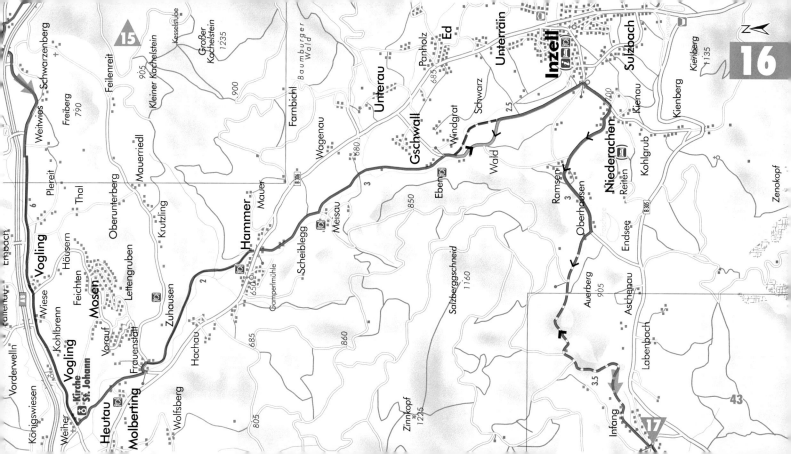

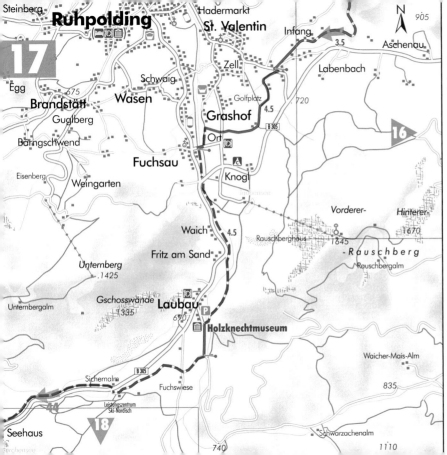

Ruhpolding

17

Steinberg · Egg · Brandstätt · Guglberg · Bärngschwend · Eisenberg · Weingarten · Hadermarkt · St. Valentin · Infang · Aschenau · Zell · Labenbach · Schwaig · Wasen · Golfplatz · Grashof · Ort · Fuchsau · Knogl · Waich · Fritz am Sand · Vorderer- · Hinterer- · Rauschberghaus · Rauschberg · Rauschbergalm · Unternberg · Gschosswände · Laubau · Holzknechtmuseum · Unternbergalm · Waicher-Mais-Alm · Sichernalm · Fuchswiese · Leistungszentrum Ski-Nordisch · Seehaus · Schwarzachenalm

16

18

905 · 3.5 · 675 · 4.5 · 720 · B 305 · 1670 · 1645 · 1425 · 1335 · 670 · B 305 · 4.5 · 835 · 740 · 1110

Biyclists near Inzell

in Salzburg. His father, Ulrich Adlgasser, a teacher, organist and sexton, taught his son at an early age to play the church organ. At the age of 15 the talented youth entered the third level at the Latin school and was accepted in the prince bishop's house chapel, where he was trained in singing, the organ, violin and Italian. At the age of 20 he became the court and cathedral organist in Salzburg, which also required him to compose chamber music and church music. Three years later he married Maria Josepha Katharina Eberlin. Her witness at the wedding was Leopold Mozart. A.C. Adlgasser and his wife then lived near the Mozart's family home in Salzburg's Getreidegasse, which led to a friendship between Adlgasser's first daughter "Victor" and W.A. Mozart's sister Nannerl. After the death of his wife, A.C. Adlgasser married twice more. Leopold Mozart again served as wedding witness at the third wedding.

Adlgasser's first oratorium dates from 1754. In 1766, after

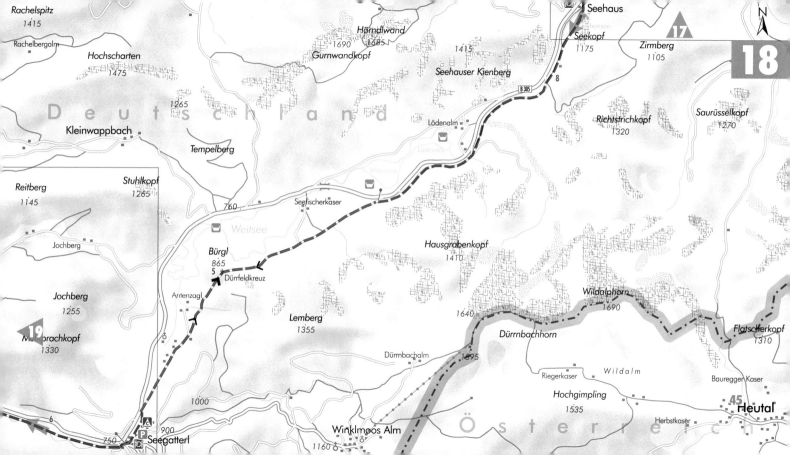

Rachelspitz
1415
Rachelbergalm
Hochscharten
1475

Hörndlwand
1690
Gurnwandkopf
1685

Seehaus
Schönsee
Seekopf
1175
Zirmberg
1105

17

18

Kleinwappbach

Tempelberg
1265

D e u t s c h l a n d

1415
Seehauser Kienberg

B 305
Lödenalm
Lodensee

8
Richtstrichkopf
1320
Saurüsselkopf
1270

Reitberg
1145
Stuhlkopf
1265

Jochberg

760

Seefischerkaser
Milbensee

Weitsee

Hausgrabenkopf
1410

Bürgl
865
5
Dürrfeldkreuz

Jochberg
1255
Antenzagl

Lemberg
1355

Wildalphorn
1690

19
Mühlprachkopf
1330

1640
Dürrnbachhorn

Flatscherkopf
1310

Dürmbachalm
1695

1000

Riegerkaser
Wildalm

Bauregger Kaser

Winklmoos Alm
1160

Hochgimpling
1535

Herbstkaser

45
Heutal

6

750
Seegatterl
900

Ö s t e r r e i c h

N

a trip to Italy, his only opera, "La Nitteti," was performed in the court theatre of the Salzburg residence. In all he wrote about 200 works, including complex sacred music and requiems, vespers, operas, oratorios and other music. At least 50 compositions were lost in the course of church secularization, but his music remained influential to the end of the 19th century. He died a few hours after suffering a stroke as he sat at the organist's bench in the Salzburg cathedral. W.A. Mozart was his successor as court and cathedral organist; Michael Haydn took over his duties at the Holy Trinity church.

Inzell to Reit im Winkl   34.5 km

Continue to the right at the main street up the steep hill and then through a curve to the left and downhill ~ and soon Niederachen comes into view.

Niederachen

Turn left on **Schmelzerstraße** ~ and then soon right on **Froschseerstraße** ~ cross a small wooden bridge and go up the hill ~ stay on the street as it curves to the left towards Froschsee and Ruhpolding ~ and continue uphill and

across several small bridges ~ where the road curves to the left turn right on the unpaved **Sulzbergweg** ~ this gravel track goes up the mountain through the forest ~ after the forest it passes a wooden hut and goes through many curves ~ now steadily downhill ~ back into the woods and more steeply downhill ~ over a small stone bridge and through a curve to the left ~ go straight at the intersection ~ the track now winds through the woods along a stream, crossing several more stone bridges ~ until it reaches the hamlet of Infang.

Infang

Continue straight out of Infang on the paved road ~ turn left at the main road ~ continue about 50 meters and then turn right on the hiking/biking trail ~ cross a stream and continue alongside the Windbach ~ cross another main road and turn left on the bike path across the wooden bridge ~ the path becomes increasingly narrow and leads under power lines ~ at the fork stay right on the narrow unpaved road ~ which leads to another bridge ~ where you turn right and then left onto the bicycle trail.

Fuchsau

The bicycle trail follows the B 305 main road ~ past the village of **Waich** ~ and soon the trail veers away from the road ~ and goes over a wooden bridge, then makes sharp left and right bends ~ at the intersection cross the bridge ~ over the stream and follow the sign to the second left ~ where the track is somewhat wider and paved with gravel ~ turn right at the next intersection ~ across the cattle guard and into the woods ~ now the track winds its way between the trees ~ when you reach the fence stay to the right.

The route runs parallel to the main road past the Bundesleistungszentrum for Ski complex ~ and follow the bicycle sign to the right ~ before the gate go right onto the asphalt under the main road and then along the right side of the road ~ continue along the bicycle path to Seehaus.

Seehaus

Stay on the bicycle path when it crosses the road and continue along the left side of the B 305 ~ ride along the **Fürchensee** ~ the bicycle path stays parallel to the main road ~ at times very close to the road ~ note the

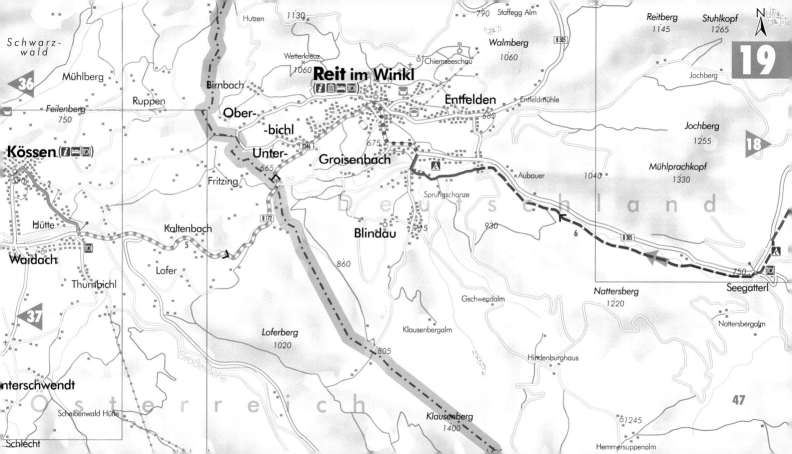

Lödensee to the right of the Bundesstraße ~ the route goes across a parking lot ~ and then over a wooden bridge, around a gate and onto a forest service road ~ which leads first past the Mittersee and then the Weitsee ~ across a series of small bridges ~ steadily uphill to the highest point at about 800 meters and then around a sharp left turn and back down the mountain.

Tip: This path is marked as the Chiemgauer MTB.

Exit the forest service road at the next gate and continue on the path along the main road ~ pass **Seegatterl** ~ and a campground and then across another parking lot ~ over a wooden bridge and further along a farm road ~ around another gate and back into the forest ~ keep the stream to the right and soon the path returns to the Bundesstraße ~ uphill through a combination left-right turn ~ to the right across the bridge and then turn onto the Bundesstraße to ride into Reit im Winkl.

Reit im Winkl

Postal code: D-83237; Telephone area code: 08640

🚺 **Tourist Information,** Rathausplatz 1, ✆ 800-20 or ✆ 800-21

🏛 Local history museum, Weitseestr. 11, Open: June-Sept, Fri 14-16 or by appointment.

🏛 **Ski museum,** Schulweg 1, ✆ 80040, Open: Mon, Thurs 15-18.

🎭 **Bauerntheater,** ✆ 800-20 or ✆ 80021

🏊 **Schwimmstadl,** ✆ 800-20 or ✆ 800-21, Open: outdoor pool daily 8:30-19; Indoor pool Tues-Sat 10-20, Sun, Mon 13-19.

🚲 **Sport Mühlberger,** Chiemseestr. 15, ✆ 985013

The climatic health resort Reit im Winkl offers a rich variety of activities and is a popular holiday destination in both summer and winter. The range of summer sports ranges from bicy-cling and hiking to golf and kite flying to rides in hot air balloons and horse-drawn wagons. In the winter months visitors can participate in the usual winter sports or take horse-drawn sleigh rides, go ice climbing and cross-country skiing. The town also has theatrical and musical entertainment, seasonal festivals, restaurants serving typical Bavarian food and a number of cafés, bars and discotheques.

In the town follow signs for Kössen ~ head uphill after a curve to the right ~ and stay right on the main road through town ~ then to the left towards Kufstein/Kössen ~ stay on Dorfstraße through the curve around the church ~ and continue to the right towards Kufstein and Kössen.

Tip: It is a short and easy ride from Reit to Kössen, and if you continue towards Kranzach you quickly pick up the main route of the Mozart Bike Trail. Take Straße 2346, which is the B 172 on the German side of the border, and follow it to Hütte. There one can turn right towards Kössen and continue through Erlau, Grundharting and Ried directly to Kranzach. The route description is continued on page 84.

Laufen to Rosenheim

143 km

The third stage of the tour begins in Laufen and heads through the Chiemgau, a part of southern Bavaria that Mozart was also familiar with. There is documentary proof that he visited Waging, the Chiemsee and Wasserburg. The Mozart Bike Trail proceeds to Waging and then on to the Chiemsee, the town of Amerang and then Wasserburg with its noteworthy historic center located on a peninsula formed by a loop in the river Inn. This stage ends in Rosenheim, where locals said the "world starts here" when the first train service to the town started in 1857.

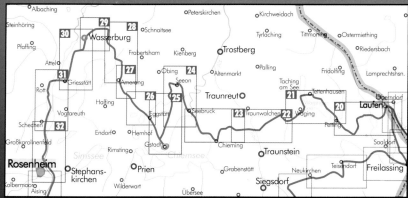

The route follows paved farm service roads and quiet country lanes, with a few unpaved stretches on the Chiemsee and along the Inn. Traffic is almost always light, with a few exceptions after Breitbrunn am Chiemsee or near Wasserburg. The route is hilly, but most of the climbs are short and mild.

Laufen to Petting   17.5 km

Starting from Laufen, after the gate turn right at the intersection and follow the road ~ past the **Gasthaus Kronprinz** ~ and then turn left towards Waging/Abtsee ~ and up the steep hill ~ turn left on **Abtsdorfer Straße** towards the cemetery ~ ride under the rail line ~ a pedestrian/biking path starts on the left side of the road ~ ride through **Oberhaslach** which is soon followed by Oberheining.

Oberheining

Take the main road through Oberheining and rejoin the bicycle path that starts on the right side at the edge of town ~ gently down hill with a fine view of the **Abtsee** ~ turn right at the junction towards Leobendorf, using the cycle path on the right side of the road ~ the lake is to the left ~ pass the beach and the clinic ~ and stay on the bike path to Leobendorf.

Leobendorf

Uphill on the main right-of-way ~ cross the road at the bus stop and go to **Bergstraße** ~ head left up the hill and then back down towards **Stögen** ~ and stay on this road past Stögen

~ skirt the farms at **Ehemoosen** as well ~ at the last farm in Ehemoosen turn right towards **Kafling** ~ at this intersection turn left onto the unpaved track ~ turn right at the next opportunity, towards Geisbach ~ turn right just before Geisbach, onto the paved road.

Geisbach

Ride past Geisbach ~ after passing the village turn left towards Knall ~ and ride through the landscape known as the **Schönramer Filz** ~ before reaching the right-of-way road, turn right onto an unpaved track ~ pass a body of water to the right ~ turn left at the T-intersection in the woods ~ and proceed to the paved main road ~ and turn right towards **Schönram**.

Schönram

In Schönram turn right on the main road towards Waging ~ a pedestrian/biking path starts at the edge of town on the right side of the road ~ stay on this path through **Wasserbrenner and Neuhaus** ~ turn right at the intersection towards Petting ~ the cycle path ends at the edge of town.

Petting

Postal code: D-83367; Telephone area code: 08686

🅸 **Tourist-Information**, Hauptstr. 13, ☎ 200

The earliest recorded mention of Petting dates to the year 1048, when it was called "Pettinga." The name denotes a place that is subject to the inflow and outflow of water, suggesting that the location may once have been an island created by the last ice age. The town originally belonged to the district around Laufen, but it later joined Waging a. See, Taching and Wonneberg to form a common administrative entity. Since 1986, however, it has been an independent community.

Petting to Waging   11.5 km

Ride past the playing fields, the church and the cemetery ~ turn right at the T-intersection, onto **Seestraße** ~ a pedestrian/bicycle path is on the right side of the road ~ take the bridge across the river Götzing ~ the bicycle path is next to the road ~ occasionally the path veers away from the road and goes into the woods ~ but mostly it runs parallel to the TS 23 ~ just before Kühnhausen the path switches to the other side of the road.

Kühnhausen

Through the village and then past the outskirts of **Lampolding** ~ and up hill to Kronwitt.

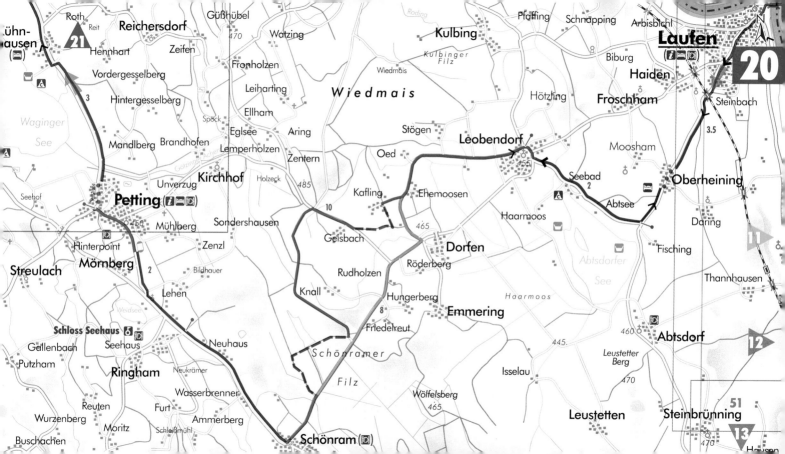

Kronwitt

After the church at Kronwitt, turn left towards Wolkersdorf.

Wolkersdorf

In Wolkersdorf ride past the church and stay left towards Horn ~ follow the road through the curve past the houses at Horn ~ and proceed straight ahead to Tettenhausen ~ turn left on the Bundesstraße ~ which has moderately heavy traffic.

Tettenhausen

Follow the main road through Tettenhausen towards Waging ~ it goes through a curve to the left and downhill to the bridge between the **Waginger See** and the **Tachinger See** ~ before the bridge go to the left and onto the bicycle bridge across the water ~ after the bridge stay on the bike trail ~ at the intersection with the stop sign turn left on the bike path and ride underneath the main road.

After crossing to the right side of the road proceed on the bicycle trail ~ at the crossing for the Seeteufel beach go straight on the side street ~ and under the main road ~ proceed past the beach into a small woods ~ stay on

Tachinger See

the marked bicycle trail to **Fisching** ~ ride through Fisching on the streets named **Zum Seeteufel** and **Kurhausstraße** ~ go straight to the intersection at the far end of the big campground ~ turn right and ride up the short hill towards Waging.

Waging am See

Postal code: D-83329; Telephone area code: 08681

🛈 **Tourist Info**, Salzburger Str. 32, ✆ 313

🏛 **Bajuwaren Museum**, Salzburger Str. 32, ✆ 45870, Open: May-Oct, Tues-Sun 10-18, Nov-April, Fri-Sun 10-18. Exhibits and artifacts about the Bajuwaren tribe.

🛏 **Karsauskeite**, Traunsteiner Str. 2, ✆ 233

🛏 **Schmuck**, Wilhelm-Scharnow-Str. 9, ✆ 222

On September 23, 1777 Wolfgang Amadeus Mozart and his mother began a concert tour bound for Paris. Their trip was also a mission to find employment because the Archbishop Colloredo had recently dismissed young Mozart and his father. In the first letter that Wolfgang Amadeus Mozart wrote on this trip he reported on his visit to Waging, saying he and his mother were being treated like princes, and that they had visited the priest Joseph Mayr and told him of their dismissal by the archbishop.

The area around Waging was first settled by the Celts, followed by the Romans and then the original Bavarians, of Bajuvaren. It was they who gave the town its name, in honor of a Bajuwar leader named Wago. Towards the end of the 14th century the town received its market right. Waging suffered no damage during the Thirty Years War, but was affected by the war of the Austrian succession and the Napoleonic campaigns.

Many refugees from the upheavals of World War Two and its aftermath also came to Waging and built new lives here. Today it is a popular holiday destination, in part thanks to its official status as a climatic health resort.

Waging to Sondermoning   18 km

At the end of **Strandbadallee** turn right towards the center of town ~ past the Rathaus on the left ~ turn right, then left ~ and proceed up **Bahnhofstraße** ~ at the filling station turn left on **Traunsteiner Straße** ~ and go straight ~ leave the village of Weidach and cross the railroad before entering a woods ~ after the woods bear left and then straight ahead to the intersection with Staatsstraße ~ straight over the crossing road and up the hill to Unteraschau.

Unteraschau

Cross the railroad and proceed towards Traunstein ~ ride through **Oberaschau** ~ turn right on the main road ~ and continue through a number of small hamlets like **Hochreit and Oed**.

Tip: Here you start to see signs for the Chiemsee-Waginger See bicycle route.

In **Straß** turn left on the main road ~ and ride uphill towards Kammer.

Kammer

In Kammer turn left on the main road towards Traunstein ~ and immediately turn

right on **Neuhausener Straße** towards Aiging ~ and ride downhill about one kilometer to Neuhausen.

Neuhausen

Stay on the main road ~ downhill on a curvy road through the woods ~ along a stream and through **Kaltenbach** ~ and then cross the Traun river before riding into Aiging.

Aiging

In Aiging the road makes many curves as it goes uphill ~ curve left on the main street and then to the right ~ straight ahead where the street curves to the left ~ depart Aiging in the direction of Nußdorf 2 kilometers away ~ the railroad tracks and the Bundesstraße run paral-

lel to the left of the trail ~ soon the route turns left and passes under the tracks and the B 304 ~ steeply uphill on the road to Nußdorf ~ over a hill and into the village.

Nußdorf/Chiemgau
Postal code: D-83365; Tel. area code: 08669

🛈 **Tourist Information, Gemeindeverwaltung,** Dorfplatz 15, ✆ 87370

In Nußdorf take the main street towards **Chieming** ~ at the edge of the village pick up the pedestrian/biking path on the left side of the road ~ continue to Sondermoning ~ at the T-intersection turn left on the larger road and proceed on the bicycle path.

Sondermoning

Sondermoning to Seeon   18 km

The bike path ends in the village ~ turn right here ~ at the intersection at the far end of Sondermoning continue straight towards Egerer ~ before reaching Egerer turn left on the unpaved road.

Egerer

Ride through Egerer ~ to the heavily-traveled Bundesstraße ~ cross the busy road and take the bicycle path on the right side of the street

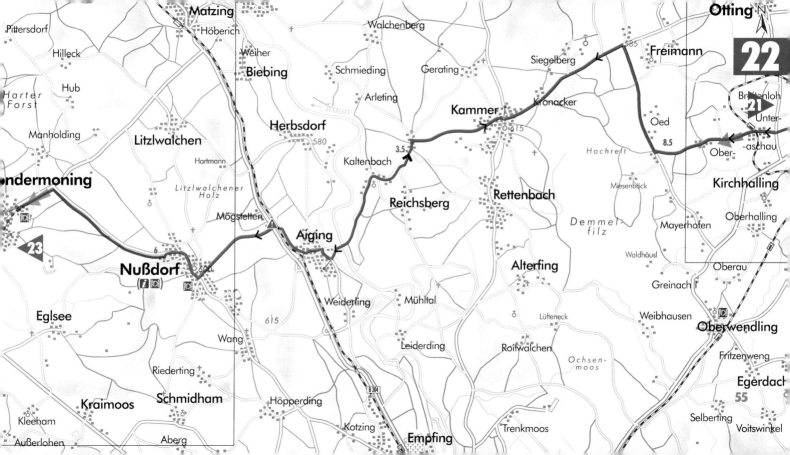

towards Pfaffing ∽ the bike path ends at the edge of town where the cemetery is ∽ turn right towards **Stöttham**.

Tip: If you proceed straight here instead of turning right you come directly to the Chieming town beach.

Chieming

Postal code: D-83339; Telephone area code: 08664

🄫 **Tourist information Chieming,** ✆ 9886-47.

🄫 **Chiemsee Infocenter,** Felden 10, D-83223 Bernau am Chiemsee, ✆ 08051/96555-0. Information about the entire Chiemsee region.

⚓ **Chiemsee Schifffahrt,** ✆ 08051/6090. Passenger ferries to Prien am Chiemsee at 9:40, 11:30, 14:15, 16:50 and 18:30. Bicycles may be transported only under limited conditions. Bicycle riding is not allowed on the islands.

🄵 **Ising pilgrimage church treasure chamber,** ✆ 08667/690. Paintings, sculptures, religious artifacts from the sacristy. May be viewed by appointment.

⚹ **Balloon rides over the** Chiemgau: N. Schneider, Stöttham, ✆ 08664/463; TS Ballonfahrten, Chieming Egerer, ✆ 8118; Hotel Gut Ising, ✆ 08667/790; Hotel Jonathan, Chieming-Hart, ✆ 08669/79090.

🚲 Bicycle rental **Chieming,** at the Minigolf, ✆ 927706.

Chieming is located directly on Bavaria's Chiemsee on the path of the Roman Juvavum–Augusta–Vindelicorum (Salzburg–Augsburg) military road. Today it retains its small-village character even though it has become a popular destination for holiday makers and tourists. Visitors can choose from a wide variety of outdoor and indoor activities, including swimming, hiking, biking, beach volleyball, golf, horseriding and much more. The village also organizes a full schedule of happenings like beach parties, wine and woods festivals and outdoor events. It is possible to rent boats or explore the Chiemsee on excursion steamers or even on the nightly dance cruises. Guided tours are also available, be they hiking tours into the nearby mountains or bike rides around the town and lake. Numerous cafés and restaurants enable visitors to relax or restore their energy after the day's exertions.

The Chiemsee

The Chiemsee and the dozens of smaller lakes that lie to its north were created by the Inn Glacier in the last Ice Age. The retreating ice left a hilly landscape dominated by moraines and basins that filled with water. Originally the Chiemsee was larger, but much of it has turned to swamps or been drained for cultivation or settlement.

Even so wetlands comprise much of the land around the Chiemsee. Its major tributaries include the Tiroler Achen – its delta at the southern end of the Chiemsee is a nature preserve – and the Prien River. The lake is drained by the Alz River flowing from the northern end at Seebruck. The Chiemsee covers about 80 square kilometers, and has a maximum depth of 74 meters. The lake's islands were first settled in the 7th and 8th centuries. It was not until the early 19th century, when the "Chiemsee painters" of Munich discovered the lake, and helped that it became an important destination for travelers and tourists.

From **Stöttham** follow signs towards **Schützing** ∽ at the last buildings in Schützing proceed on the unpaved track ∽ past the **Neubauer** farm ∽ and use the unpaved track along the shore of the Chiemsee to reach **Arlaching** on the way to Seebruck ∽ in Seebruck turn into **Haushoferstraße** ∽ and then turn right on the bicycle path along the Alz to Truchtlaching.

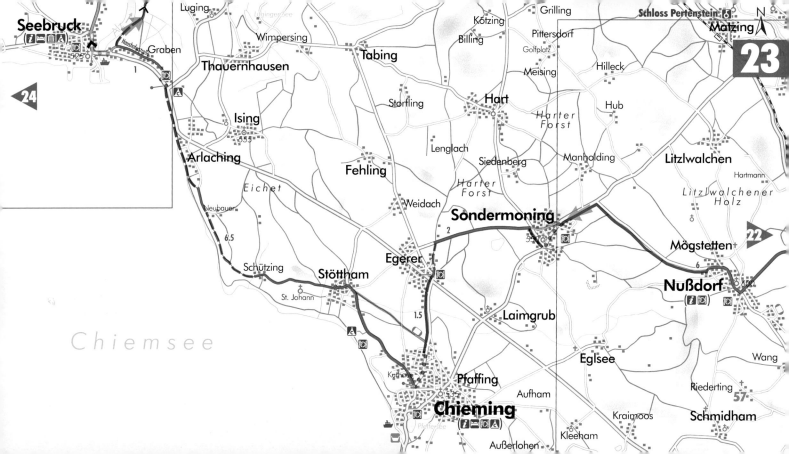

Seebruck

Luging

Graben

Thauernhausen

Wimpersing

Tabing

Grilling

Kötzing

Billing

Pittersdorf

Schloss Pertenstein

Matzing

23

Golfplatz

Meising

Hilleck

Ising

Hart

Storfling

Hub

Harter Forst

Manholding

Litzlwalchen

Arlaching

Lenglach

Siedenberg

Hartmann

Fehling

Eichet

Harter Forst

Litzlwalchener Holz

Neubauer

Weidach

Sondermoning

6.5

2

Mögstetten

Schützing

Egerer

6

St. Johann

Stöttham

Nußdorf

1.5

Chiemsee

Laimgrub

Kathaus

Pfaffing

Eglsee

Wang

Chieming

Aufham

Riederting

57

Pfaffersee

Kraimoos

Schmidham

Außerlohen

Kleeham

24

1

N

Seebruck

Postal code: D-83358; Telephone area code: 08667

ℹ Tourist Information Seebruck, ✆ 7139

🏛 Bedaium Roman museum, Römerstr. 3., ✆ 7503, Open: Oct-April and May-Sept, Tues-Sat 10-17, Sun 13-17. Museum with archaeological finds and artifacts from prehistoric times to the 1st and 2nd centuries AD

Seebruck was established about 50 AD by the Romans. Originally named Bedaium, it served as a military camp along the Juvavum–Augusta–Vindelicorum (Salzburg–Augsburg) military road. Over the course of time its name changed to Pontena, followed by Prucca and finally to its current name Seebruck. Today it is an officially recognized climatic resort and home to the Chiemsee's largest marina for pleasure boats.

Proceed along the Alz uphill towards **Stöffling** ~ *turn left towards Truchtlaching* ~ *and pass the Celtic farm and enter the town.*

Truchtlaching

At the church turn left towards Seeon and across the Alz onto the new bicycle path to **Döging-Poing** *and Seeon* ~ *pass the playing fields and ride into Seeon.*

Lake near Roitham

Seeon

Postal code: D-83370; Telephone area code: 08624

ℹ Cultural and education center, Klosterweg 1, ✆ 8970

⛪ Seeon monastery

⛪ St. Nikolaus chapel, built in 1757. Noteworthy are the stucco decorations by Johann Michael Feichtmayer and frescos by Joseph Hartmann. Tours only by appointment. Information at the cultural and education center.

⛪ St. Lambert, the monastery church was first built in the late 11th century, and then rebuilt about 100 years later. Noteworthy for its Renaissance frescos, tombstones of various abbots, its cloister and the "Madonna with Child" painting.

The monastery at Seeon was founded in 994 by the Pfalzgraf Arbio I. Because the original build-ings were deemed too small and primitive, a new monastery was built at the end of the 11th century. The Benedictine Order established a writing school that produced documents for the Seeon monastery as well as for other monasteries and churches in the region. After the takeover of church properties during secularization, the monastery was used as a residence by various noble families. Wolfgang Amadeus Mozart also came to the monastery on occasion to compose his music in peace. Later it was used as a spa, a resort and a military barracks. In 1986 the Upper Bavaria regional government purchased the site and undertook major renovations. Today it is available for concerts, exhibitions, workshops and conferences as well as private functions like weddings.

Seeon to Breitbrunn   15.5 km

Take **Weinbergstraße** ~ *to the Bräuhausen church* ~ *which offers a terrific view of the Seeon monastery* ~ *take the Klostersteg to the monastery and continue straight* ~ *at the large parking lot turn left onto the unpaved narrow track to Grünweg* ~ *pass a farm on a farm service track* ~ *past a small pond* ~ *that asphalt ends where the pond begins.*

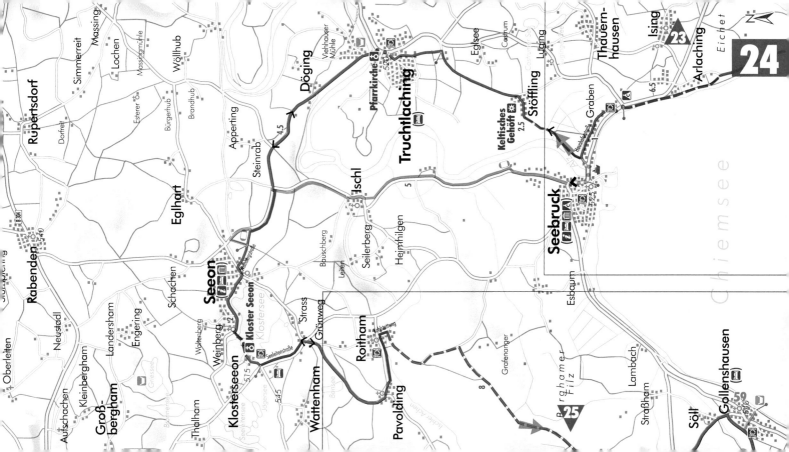

Seeon monastery

Turn left when you come to the main road ~ cross a bridge and then make a sharp right turn ~ to where a pedestrian/biking path starts on the right side ~ take this to Roitham.

Roitham

At the church go down to the right onto **Kohlstattweg** ~ and proceed towards Stetten ~ turn right before you reach the bridge ~ the asphalt ends after you pass the last houses ~ ride a short stretch through woods ~ stay left towards Fembach and Stetten ~ uphill gently on a gravel surface ~ along the edge of a forest and then into the woods ~ the path exits the forest and reaches Fembach.

Fembach

There is an asphalt road to Stetten.

Stetten

In the village turn left on the main street ~ proceed about 500 meters and take the second right ~ and ride through the forest to Söll.

Söll

Before entering Söll turn right towards Lienzing.

Tip: If you proceed straight here, you soon reach Gollenshausen, which lies directly on the Chiemsee and has a public beach.

Go straight on the main street ~ out of Gollenshausen and towards Breitbrunn ~ gently uphill to **Lienzing** ~ straight through the village on the country road and through the hamlet of Ed as well ~ gently uphill towards the forest ~ through the woods towards Breitbrunn ~ through a curve to the right and into Breitbrunn.

Breitbrunn am Chiemsee

Postal code: D-83254; Telephone area code: 08054

🄸 **Tourist Information**, Gollenhausener Str. 1, ✆ 234

Breitbrunn

🄳 **St. Johannes baroque church**, classically beautiful church on a hill over the village. Interior includes tombstone of a Chiemsee bishop.

🄴 Regarded as the oldest settlement on the Chiemsee. **Several Stone Age and Roman artifacts** on display in the **Rathaus**

Although the center of Breitbrunn does not front directly on the lake, the community has one of the Chiemsee's longest shorelines. This part of the lake is characterized by its idyllic Kailbach and Mühln coves and the peninsulas Urfahrn and Sassau. An extensive network of hiking and biking paths through a landscape of gently rolling hills, verdant meadows and fragrant woods lead to numerous scenic points and historic sites. The Langbürgner See northwest of Breitbrunn lies in a nature reserve and offers an interesting contrast to the busy Chiemsee.

Tip: The main route turns to the right at the intersection with the main street in Breitbrunn.

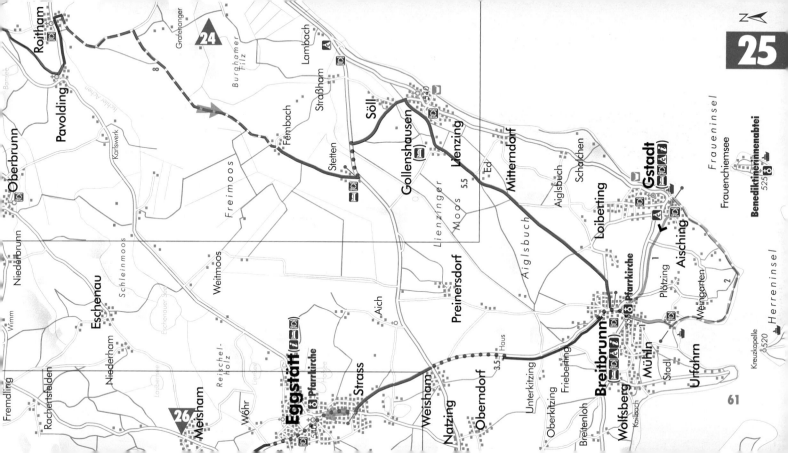

Fraueninsel in the Chiemsee

One can also turn left for a sidetrip to Gstadt, a Chiemsee resort town with a marina, hotels and inns. From Gstadt one can ride along the shoreline to Mühln and return to Breitbrunn.

Gstadt am Chiemsee

Postal code: D-83257; Telephone area code: 08054

🛈 **Tourist Information**, Seeplatz 5, ✆ 08054/442

⚓ **Chiemsee Schifffahrt**, ✆ 08051/6090. Passenger ferry departures: To the Fraueninsel every hour starting at 8:50; to the Herreninsel via Fraueninsel also at 7:20, 8:15, 10:20 and 10:50.

⑤ **Schloss Herrenchiemsee** with Ludwig II Museum, ✆ 08051/6887-0, Open: April-Sept, Mon-Sun 9-17. Unfinished copy of Versailles, built by Ludwig II on the Herreninsel. Can be reached by ship from Prien/Stock and Gstadt.

⑥ **Benedictine abbey**, Frauenwörth on the Fraueninsel, ✆ 08054/9070, Open: Whitsun to end of Sept, Mon-Sun 11-18. Michaels chapel with byzantine frescos.

At the intersection with the main road in Breitbrunn turn right towards Eggstätt.

Breitbrunn to Amerang   15 km

Take the main route towards Eggstätt ~ by simply following the road north from Breitbrunn ~ a pedestrian/bike path starts at the edge of town on the left side of the road ~ the path ends in Haus. Continue on the roadway ~ in **Weisham** proceed straight on Route 2095 with less traffic to Eggstätt.

Eggstätt

Postal code: D-83125; Telephone area code: 08056

🛈 **Tourist Info**, Obinger Str. 7, ✆ 1500

⑧ **St. Georg parish church**, neogothic church built on older foundations. Roman tombstone.

⑨ **"Unterwirt" inn**, ✆ 337

The earliest known mention of Eggstätt dates to the year 925, but the area was settled much earlier. A Roman road probably passed near the present site of Eggstätt. The 13th century upper

Herrenchiemsee castle

Bavarian town of Urbar is regarded as the direct predecessor of what is today Eggstätt. Over the course of the centuries the town belonged to various local entities, and it has been an independent municipality only since 1986. It lies in Bavaria's oldest and largest nature preserve, the Eggstätt-Hemhofer lakes district. This unique ecosystem created during the last Ice Age includes a labyrinth of lakes, moors, meadows and flood plain forests that support a variety of rare plants and animals. It can be explored on a network of hiking and biking trails.

In Eggstätt follow the main road to the right towards Halfing/Obing ~ then stay left towards Hartsee-Halle and Obing ~ pass to the left of the church ~ note the Hartsee to the left after leaving the town limits ~ use the pedestrian/hiking path on the right side of the roadway ~ go straight at the intersection ~ the bicycle path ends for a short piece.

The bicycle path resumes at the next intersection ~ pass the **Pelhamer See** as you ride through **Unterulsham** ~ gently uphill through a long curve to the right ~ after passing through **Oberulsham turn left towards** Gachensolden ~ take the bike path next to the road to **Sägwirt**, where the path ends and continue on the country lane to Gachensolden.

Gachensolden

At the main junction turn right towards Halfing and Höslwang ~ turn left at the T-intersection outside Höslwang ~ and then right at the next junction and into **Höslwang.**

Höslwang

8 St. Nikolaus baroque church with rococo in-

terior. For centuries the church belonged to the diocese of Salzburg.

After the church turn left on **Ameranger Straße** ~ a bike path starts on the left side of the road at the edge of town ~ proceed through **Obergebertsham** ~ the bike path ends at the next junction ~ stay on the road through a small forest on the way to Oberratting.

Oberratting

Amerang is two kilometers to the north ~ the road goes down a steep hill ~ which offers a fine view of Amerang ~ take the main road to the right over the railroad ~ and enter Amerang.

Amerang

Postal code: D-83123; Telephone area code: 08075

ℹ **Tourist Info Amerang**, Bahnhofstr. 3, ℘ 9197-28, www.amerang.de

🏛 **Farmhouse museum**, Im Hopfgarten 2, ℘ 915090, Open: Mid March-mid Nov, Tues-Sun 9-18 (doors open until 17), closed

27

Mondays. Evolution of farm living, production and crafts. Original artifacts representing five centuries of Bavarian rural life.

🏛 **Automobile museum**, Wasserburger Str. 38, ☎ 8141, Open: Tues-Sun 10-18 (doors open until 17), from 1 Nov-31 March only open Sundays and holidays. Automobile collection with 220 German motorcars dating from 1886 to the contemporary. Also a large-scale model railroad with about 650 meters of track.

🏰 **Schloss Amerang**, ☎ 91920, Guided tours early June-early Sept, daily 10, 11, 12, 13 and 14. Also open on request. Castle dates to 1072. Today serves as venue for concerts and events. Includes museum and tours.

🏰 **St. Rupert Amerang parish church**, single knave gothic church dating to 1367. Expanded in 1506 and 1958. Baroque renovation and decoration according to the Aiblinger style around 1700. Earlier styles evident in the baptistery.

🏰 **Meilham church**, 1.5 kilometers south-east of Schloss Amerang. 12th century church was redesigned by the Laimingers around 1500.

🚲 **"Zum Steinbauer"**, Forellenweg 8, ☎ 211

🔧 **"Radl-Ladl"**, Sebastian Thusbass, Obinger Str. 7, ☎ 1698

Amerang is noted for the well-known castle of the same name. The earliest recorded mention of the castle dates to 1072. Over the centuries it has served as the family seat for the Scaligers, followed by the counts Lamberg and currently the barons Crailsheim. During the summer months

Eggstätt from above

the castle hosts regular concerts. Guided tours are available. The castle may also be hired for private functions.

Amerang to Wasserburg   19.5 km

Ride past the left side of the church and follow signs for Wasserburg ↝ pass the playing fields and then follow the stream ↝ turn right at the "Alt Rhodos" restaurant ↝ cross a bridge and pass the automobile museum ↝ the next village is **Kammer** ↝ stay to the left at the junction in **Asham, towards** Halfurt.

Halfurt

In Halfurt cross a bridge and turn right ↝ ride along the edge of the forest towards Unteröd.

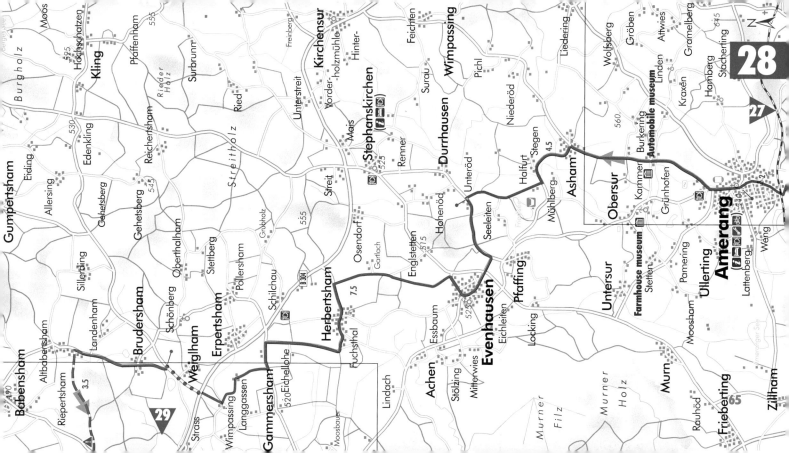

Wasserburg from above

Unteröd
Turn left at the main road, towards Evenhausen ～ followed by a right turn to Evenhausen.

Evenhausen
Ride through Evenhausen ～ at the church turn right towards Englstetten ～ turn left before you reach the T-intersection ～ proceed through the hamlet of **Gartlach** ～ turn left at the T-intersection to Herbertsham and Fuchsthal.

Herbertsham
Ride through the entire village ～ take the sharp right turn at the far edge of the village and proceed to the next T-intersection ～ turn left

and then take the first right ～ through the hamlet of **Wimpassing** ～ then a sharp right and up to the **B 304** main road ～ straight across the B 304 and onto the moderately busy road towards Kling ～ turn left towards Brudersham.

Brudersham
Ride through the village towards Altbabensham.

Altbabensham
Make the sharp left turn at the bicycle sign ～ past house number 14 ～ the asphalt comes to an end and the track gets bumpy ～ the track gets narrower in the forest ～ cross the main road at the edge of the woods ▲ Caution: Dangerous intersection! ～ ride through **Riepertsham** and turn left on the main road towards Penzing.

Penzing
Postal code: D-83547; Telephone area code: 08071
🛈 **Town office**, Babensham, Raiffeisenstr. 3, ☎ 9220-0
Turn right in the center of Penzing, across from the small palace ～ after a short distance turn left to Neudeck.

Neudeck
Follow the main road towards Wasserburg ～ after a short stretch through a forest you come to Staatsstraße ～ turn right on the bicycle path.

Rathaus in Wasserburg

Tip: After about 100 meters arrive at an intersection where you have the option of turning right and going into the old center of Wasserburg. To do so follow signs for the "Altstadt". To bypass Wasserburg ride through the underpass and follow signs for **Weikertsham**.

Wasserburg am Inn
Postal code: D-83512; Telephone area code: 08071
🛈 **Tourism office Stadt Wasserburg a. Inn**, Salzsenderzeile, Rathaus, ☎ 10522, Fax 105-21, www.wasserburg.de
🏛 **Wegmacher Museum**, Herderstr. 1, ☎ 9185. Open: Mon-Fri 8-11: 30 and 13-15. About roads and traffic, from Roman times to today.
🏛 **First Imaginary Museum**, in the former Heilig Geist Spital,

✆ 4358, Open: year round Tues-Sun, 13-17, closed Mondays. Unique museum containing copies of 500 of the world's most famous paintings and drawings.

🏛 **Museum Wasserburg**, Herreng. 15, ✆ 925290, Open: 1 May-30 Sept Tues-Sun 13-17, 1 Oct-30 April Tues-Sun 13-16, closed Mondays and January. Comprehensive collection focuses on three subjects: Local history, rural living, crafts and industry. Guided tours for groups by appointment.

🔯 Castle built 1526 to 1537. Today serves as retirement home. No tours available.

✳ **Kernhaus.** Across from Rathaus. 15th century building with stucco facade by J. B. Zimmermann about 1738.

✳ **Brucktor (gate).** Entrance gate to the old town. Hidden behind the gate is the Heilig Geist Spital (1341) with its late-gothic chapel.

✳ **Tollhouse.** Bruckgasse. 14th century structure believed to be oldest house in Wasserburg.

✳ **Rathaus.** Town hall was build 1458-59. Especially noteworthy are the historic town chambers.

✉ **Badria,** Alkorstr. 14, ✆ 8133. Swimming, sports and recreation center.

Wolfgang Amadeus Mozart visited the city of Wasserburg on the Inn for the first time in 1763, as a seven-year old boy. The Mozarts were traveling in their own coach, accompanied by their servant Sebastian Winter. Due to a broken wheel, they arrived in the city late at night. Two days later Mozart's father showed his son how to play the foot pedals of an organ. Leopold Mozart later reported that the boy immediately played the organ as though he already had been practicing for months.

Mozart visited Wasserburg again on September 23, 1777, as he traveled with his mother. That evening he wrote to his father what is now known as the "Wasserburg letter."

Two factors have combined to give the old town of Wasserburg its unique character: one is its location on a small peninsula formed by a tight loop of the Inn River; the other is the densely built town center. The result is unquestion-

Trautbach Bärnham
Puttenham Babensham
Graben Zell ○435 Würmertsham
Sonnenholzen Stürzlham
Gschwendt
Odelsham Penzing 3.5 Riepertsham
Koblberg 2 Penzinger See
Neudeck
Wasserburg Straßloh
am Inn Brudersham
Gabersee Blaufeld Strass
Burgau Brucktor 490 Weiglham
Langwied Aich Wimpassing
Burgerfeld ○505 2.5 Weikertsham Berg Langgassen
2.5 2 Gammersham
30 Urfarn Bachmehring ○28
1 **Eiselfing**
Höhfelden Dirneck Moosbauer
5 Hafenham 485 Moosfischer
Freiham Eiselfinger See **67**
500 Alteiselfing Lindach
Spielberg

29

N

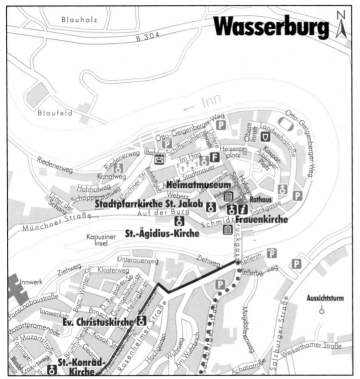

ably the most picturesque city on the Inn. The city's geography goes back to when the moraine wall holding back the Inn Glacier Lake broke, releasing the river to find its course through the hilly landscape.

Because the city center lies so near the river, it is often threatened by high-water during the annual thaw of snow in the Alps. Today a flood wall with a sculpture park protects the city from the clay-colored waters. The river also brought prosperity, however. The "salt boats" from Reichenhall to Munich passed through Wasserburg, and the Inn also connected the town to more distant centers along the Danube. Until 150 years ago, barges were pulled upstream by teams of horses – the voyage from Vienna to Wasserburg took some six weeks. Construction of the castle after which the city was named was begun in the early middle ages.

Wasserburg not only operated as Munich's harbor on the Inn River, but was also the point from which Bavarian troops were sent to battle the Turkish armies during the Battle for Vienna. The long row of buildings that front the Inn have a Mediterranean flair with Italian architectural touches brought to the region during the 30 Years War.

Wasserburg to Griesstätt   8.5 km

From Bachmehring take the main road ~ straight to **Höhfelden** ~ turn left between two houses and proceed straight to Spielberg ~ in Spielberg continue straight on **Kirchweg to the next village,** Kerschdorf.

Kerschdorf

Turn left on the main road at the inn ~ after about 200 meters turn left and then right after another 100 meters ~ straight to **Laiming** ~ through the village and then left

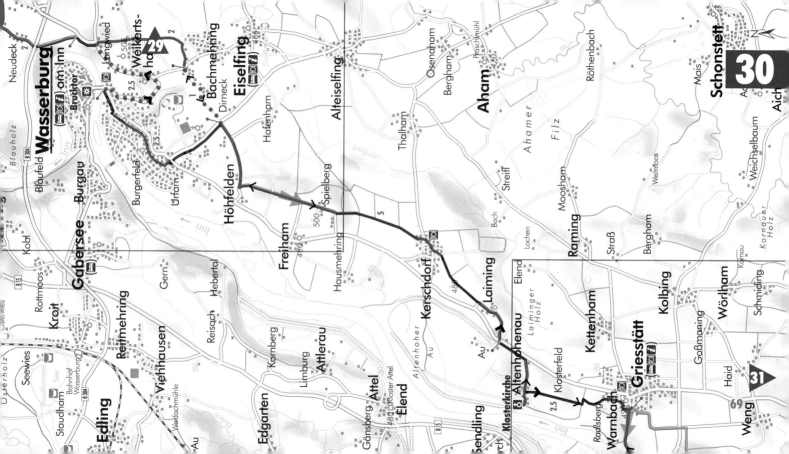

at the main road – ride 400 meters with traffic and then turn right to Altenhohenau.

Altenhohenau

The convent at Altenhohenau, founded in the 13th century, was the first Dominican convent in Germany. Over the centuries the nuns there suffered a series of disasters and hardships, including fire, flight to the Frauenchiemsee from invading Swedish troops, and more than one-hundred years of closure during secularization of the church. The convent's church includes an altar by Ignaz Günther and the "Altenhohenau Jesulein," a carved figure dressed in clothes which was believed to possess miraculous powers. The rococo interior of the church is also noteworthy.

Just before the convent church, the route turns south through Klosterfeld to Griesstätt – turn right after the cemetery.

Tip: In **Griesstätt** you have the option of taking the Inn River Bike Trail to Rosenheim. A more detailed description of the route can be found in the *bikeline*-Radtourenbuch Inn Radweg 2, from Innsbruck to Passau (available in German).

Griesstätt

Postal code: 83556; Telephone area code: 08039

Town office, Innstr. 4, ✆ 9056-0

Griesstätt was officially recognized for the first time in the "Rhini Urkunde," a document issued in 924 by Herzog Arnulf von Bayern. Members of the lower nobility lived in Griesstätt since the 12th century, and over time emerged as the town's permanent rulers. In the 16th century the town passed to Sieghart von Leublfing, who sold the Hofmark to Alexander von Freyberg zu Hohenaschenau and Neubeuern. The Altenhohenau convent purchased Griesstätt in 1667. After the secularization of church property, Griesstätt joined the tax district with Holzhausen and Kolbing. In 1986 Griesstätt was granted the status of an independent municipality.

Griesstätt to Rosenheim   19.5 km

Take the main road out of Griesstätt – to the bridge over the River Inn – turn right and cross the river and then turn left onto the gravel path – and ride past the confluence of the Rott stream as it meets the Inn – at the junction with another track turn left across the bridge and follow the curve to the right along the dam next to the Rott stream – after about 2 kilometers turn left and cross the Rott.

Tip: At the bridge one also has the option of turning left and making a sidetrip to Rott am Inn, where one can view the Kaiser crypt in the Benedictine church.

Rott am Inn

Postal code: D-83543; Telephone area code: 08039

Gemeindeverwaltung Rott am Inn, Kaiserhof 3, ✆ 9068-0.

Benedictine church and Kaiser crypt. A masterpiece of Bavarian baroque architecture, built 1759-63 according to a design by Johann Michael Fischer. It is also the burial place of Bavaria's long-time post-war state premier, Franz Josef Strauss, and his wife.

In the 11th century the Benedictine order established an abbey at Rott am Inn. The order's holdings at times comprised up to 65 properties that reached as far as the lower Danube. The older abbey structures were lost during the secularization of church properties in the 19th century, but the church remains. This impressive example of upper Bavarian baroque architecture shows the transition from the rococo to classicism. The interior is completely intact and includes works by many of the period's leading artists. The ceiling painting was done by Matthäus Günter.

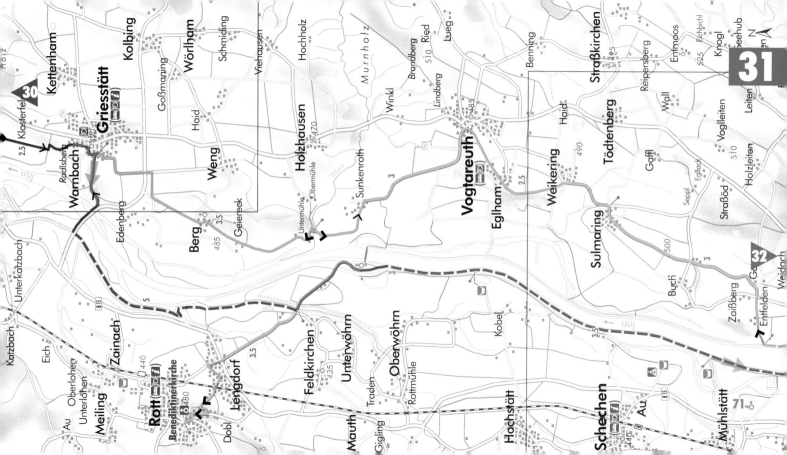

The abbey in Rott am Inn is just one of many abbeys that grace the river and have helped establish the Inn Valley's reputation as a "land of culture."

The main route bears to the left towards the Inn ~ then curves around the power plant at **Vogtareuth** ~ and continues on an unpaved track upstream along the Inn ~ the bicycle trail to Rosenheim is 13 kilometers long ~ and passes several small swimming lakes ~ ride into Rosenheim and soon cross the confluence of the Mangfall and the Inn ~ cross the Mangfall ~ by turning left on **Innstraße** and riding across the bridge.

Rosenheim

Postal code: D-83022, .24, .26; Telephone area code: 08031

🛈 **Tourism info**, am Ticketcenter, Stollstraße1, Postadresse: D-83022 Kufsteiner Str. 4, ✆ 3659061.

🏛 **Inn museum**, Innstr. 74, ✆ 305148, Open: April-Oct, Fri 9-12, Sat/Sun 10-16. Exhibits about hydrology and geology of the Inn, the history of its settlement and development, and river travel. Model of a train of barges being hauled upstream.

🏛 **City Gallery**, Max-Brahm-Pl., ✆ 36-1447, Open: Tues-Sun 10-17 and every 1st, 3rd and 5th Sunday of the month. Closed Mondays and Fridays. Rotating exhibitions

🏛 **City Museum**, Mittertor, Ludwigspl. 26, ✆ 798994, Open: Tues-Sat 10-17 and every 1st, 3rd and 5th Sunday of the month 13-17. Exhibits on prehistoric and ancient times, Roman artifacts, Inn river navigation, market history, crafts and industry. Includes a complete 17th/18th century kitchen, religious folk art and contemporary art.

🏛 **Wood technology Museum**, Max-Josefs-Pl. 4, ✆ 16900, Open: Tues-Sat 10-17, every 2nd and 4th Sunday of the month 13-17. Uses of wood for homes, farming, transportation, architecture and art. Original pieces and models.

🏛 **Lokschuppen** exhibition center. Rathausstr. 24, ✆ 3659036. Open: Mon-Fri, 9-18, Sat, Sun, Hol 10:30-18 (alternate opening times possible). Special exhibitions between May-Nov.

✴ **Max-Josefs-Platz**. The pedestrian area in the old town has numerous typical Inn city houses with their covered loggias and horizontal facade tops that hide "V" shaped roofs.

✴ **Mittertor**, historic 14th century city gate.

The city of Rosenheim occupies a mound of gravel left by a prehistoric lake that was drained after the last Ice Age. The rivers Mangfall and Inn now run through this basin, which lies some 450 meters above sea-level.

In early Roman times the site of Rosenheim lay at the crossroads of important trade routes: the consular road between Salzburg and Augsburg and the road from Innsbruck to Regensburg. Even before the year 15 B.C., when the Roman Emperor Augustus conquered the region and divided it into the Provinces of Noricum and Rätien, traders brought amber and other goods through the region on their way to markets in southern and northern Europe.

Today Rosenheim is still an important trading center. The city on the Inn River remains an economic engine for an area that extends far beyond its own borders. In 1857 residents of the Chiemgau declared that "the world starts in Rosenheim" when the first train rolled into the city.

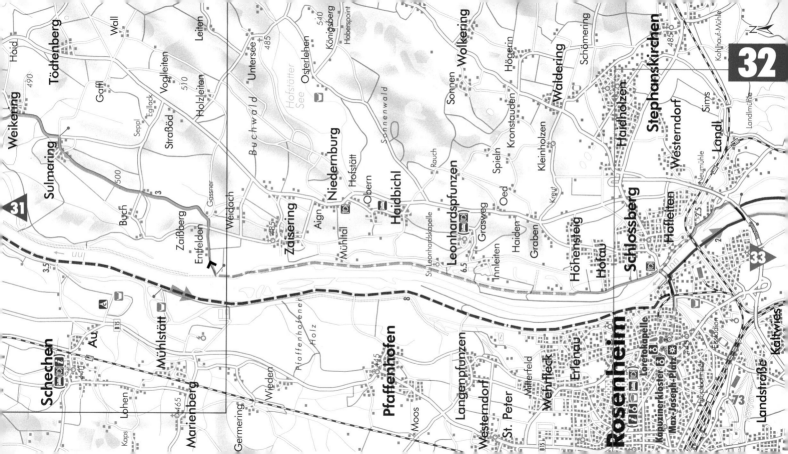

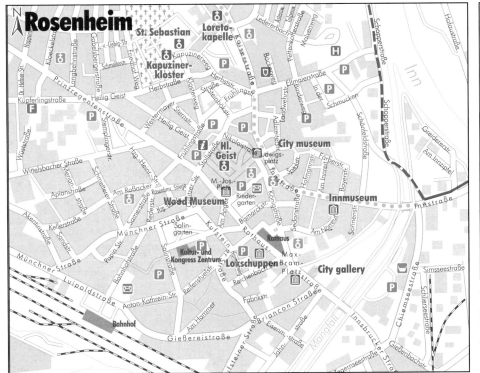

Rosenheim

St. Sebastian
Loreto-kapelle
Kapuziner-kloster
Heilig Geist
Hl. Geist
City museum
Wood Museum
Innmuseum
Kultur- und Kongress Zentrum
Lokschuppen
Rathaus
City gallery
Max-Bram-Platz
Bahnhof

City of Rosenheim

The line from Munich to Vienna had originally planned to go through Wasserburg, but during construction a route through Rosenheim was chosen.

From Rosenheim to Salzburg

The fourth segment of the tour begins in Rosenheim and leads up the pretty Inn Valley into the Tyrol with its breathtaking Alpine panoramas and geranium filled villages. In Bad Reichenhall the bicycle tourist must decide whether to ride through the charming Saalach Valley or proceed to Salzburg via Berchtesgaden. This final segment brings the Mozart Bike Trail back to its beginning, the city of Salzburg.

Most of the route follows bicycle trails along the Inn, quiet country lanes or farm and forest service tracks. Although there are only a few very short stretches on busier roads, the route has a number of climbs, especially in the Tyrol.

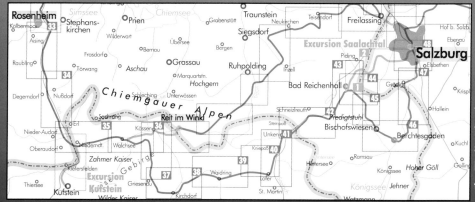

Rosenheim to Niederndorf   29.5 km

Take the Inn River bridge to the east bank and turn right on the bike path along **Rohrdorfer Straße** ~ after the tunnel under the railroad there is a bike path on the left side to the next bridge across the Inn ~ turn right and cross the bridge ~ make a loop down to the river bank ~ and continue on the asphalt on the river embankment ~ loop around the transformer station and back to the shoreline ~ the asphalt comes to an end and the track continues on gravel towards the Autobahn bridge ~ under the bridge and proceed another 4.5 kilometers along the embankment to the turnoff for Neubeuern.

Tip: Here you have the option of visiting the city and the castle Neubeuern.

Neubeuern

Postal code: D-83115; Telephone area code: 08035

🛈 **Tourism office**, Marktpl. 4, ☎ 2165.

🏛 **Inn river shipping museum**

🏰 **Schloss Neubeuern**. Built 1150 on a hilltop high over the town.

The coat of arms of Neubeuern shows two boat hooks crossed over each other. They recall former days when the town's prosperity depended on navigation of the river. Even today the church, restaurants and many of Neubeuern's buildings are decorated with images relating to river shipping. The river now plays an existential role for the town only during high-water; the last boat makers practiced their craft until fairly recently. The flat-bottomed barges built in Neubeuern – "Neubeurer Gamsen" – plied the Inn and Danube as far as distant Hungary.

The views from the terraces of the castle above Neubeuern extend far up the Inn River valley and into the foothills of the Alps. Far to the west one can see the Wendelstein, at 1,838 meters the highest mountain of the Bavarian Inn valley. Beneath the castle lies the "inner market," a charming central square surrounded by richly decorated old houses and comfortable inns that help make this one of the prettiest towns in Bavaria.

The main bicycle route stays on the embankment along the river ~ to the Nußdorf river barrage ~ the bicycle trail returns to an asphalted surface at the bridge at Nußdorf where it turns to the west for a short stretch.

Tip: On this main road you have the option of turning left for a sidetrip to Nußdorf. The town is noteworthy especially for its well-preserved village character, and for the inviting beer garden at the traditional Bavarian "Schneiderwirt" restaurant and inn.

Nußdorf am Inn

Postal code: D-83131; Telephone area code: 08034

🛈 **Tourism association**, Brannenburger Str. 10, ☎ 907920 or ☎ 19433, Fax 907921

🏰 **St. Vitus parish church**. Lindenweg. Late gothic church from the 15th century.

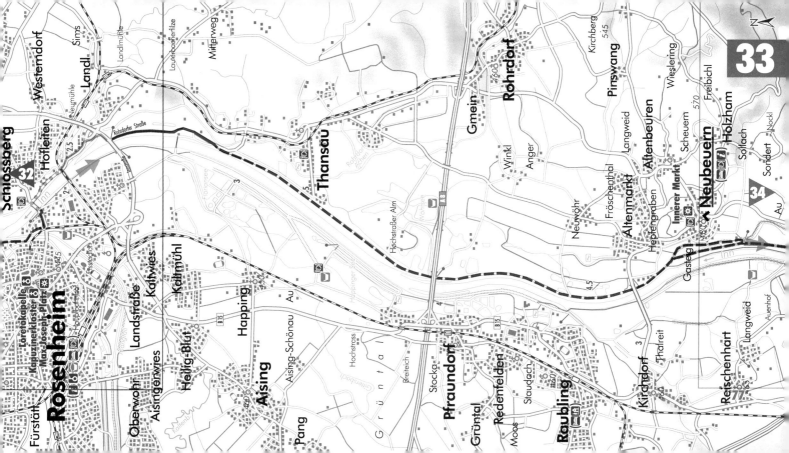

- **Kirchwald with pilgrimage chapel**, a 45-minute walk from the village. The last occupied hermitage in upper Bavaria.
- **"Der Mühlenweg" outdoor exhibition**, located along the Mühlbach. Information and displays about water-powered grain mills, a sawmill, and a smithy.

The village of Nußdorf probably obtained its name from the many nut-bearing trees in the surrounding forests. The area was originally settled by Celts, who were followed by the Romans who lived along the Innsbruck to Regensburg trade route. The earliest-known reference to the village dates from the year 788. Its main industry was the production and processing of chalk, plaster, cement, wood and charcoal. Many of the area's residents also worked as rivermen, bringing the region's goods down river as far as the Black Sea. Because Nußdorf lay directly on important transportation routes, it often fell victim to fire and pillage. After a short period when it was united with nearby Neubeuern, it today is an independent municipality with 23 districts. Information and background about the region's history and economic development can be seen at "Der Mühlenweg" outdoor museum.

In 2001 Nußdorf won the Gold Medal in the annual "Making our Village more Beautiful" competition. A sidetrip to one of Bavaria's most beautiful villages is certainly worth the time.

Before crossing the bridge turn left on the unpaved track along the Inn river embankment and proceed 8.5 kilometers to Erl — were the gravel track ends at a paved road.

Tip: Turn left for an excursion to the village of Erl.

Erl
Postal code: A-6343; Telephone area code: 05373
- **Tourism association**, ✆ 8117.
- **Trockenbachwasserfall**. East of Erl, nature preserve with spectacular waterfall.

To the left one can see the *Passionsspielhaus* of Erl, where the Passion Play is performed every six years in continuation of a tradition dating back to the early 17th century. The current theatre, a curved sail-like structure, was built in 1959 and has seating for 1,500 spectators. Its outstanding acoustics have been praised by performers such as the conductor Sergiu Celibidache.

Turn right from the unpaved path to continue along the main route — pass the indoor pool and head towards **Mühlgraben** — turn right on the main road — and proceed down the street to the Inn bridge connecting Reisach and Mühlgraben.

Tip: For an excursion to the town of Oberaudorf turn right and cross the river.

Oberaudorf
Postal code: D-83080; Telephone area code: 08033
- **Tourism info**, Kufsteiner Str. 6, ✆ 301-20
- **Burgtor museum**. Open: Tues and Fri, 14-18. Exhibits about the history and development of Oberaudorf and Inn river shipping.
- **Hocheck recreation area**, ✆ 30350, summer toboggan run, an adventure playground, and an illuminated ski piste (winter only) make this a popular destination.
- **Luegsteinsee public beach**, open daily May-Sept.

The tourism industry in Oberaudorf got started when a weaver by the name of Seywald purchased a former hermit's cell at the base of the Luegsteinwand cliff. According to local legend he set up shop and expanded the house before setting up an inn. The inn known as the "Gasthaus zum Weber an der Wand" soon began attracting visitors. A further attraction, the mountain inn "Zum feurigen Tatzlwurm" above Oberaudorf, was opened in 1863 and became popular among the artists around the writer Ludwig Steub. At the end of the 19th century, the area gained additional popularity through the efforts of the enterprising pharmacist Carl Hagen, who recognized the growing popularity of winter sports. Organized tourism began developing in the 1930s and helped establish Oberaudorf as one of the oldest and most important resort towns in the Bavarian Inn Valley.

The main bicycle route continues along the road towards Niederndorf ~ after about one kilometer, where the road curves to the right, take the bicycle trail that descends to the right into the flood plain ~ turn left onto the B 172

Oberaudorf

at the Tiroler Hof inn and then immediately take the first right.

Follow this path to the Jennbach stream and then turn left before crossing the stream ~ follow the stream to the next crossing street.

Tip: Here you have the option of turning left to visit the quaint small town of Niederndorf.

Niederndorf

Postal code: A-6342; Telephone area code: 05373

🅸 **Tourismusverband**, No. 32, ✆ 61377.

🅱 **Parish church.** Frescos by the painter Josef Adam Mölk were rediscovered in 1948 during church renovations.

🅲 **s'Theata Niederndorf**, Dorf 46a, ✆ 61536. Village theatre.

🅰 **Wildpark near Wildbichl**, 5 km north-east, ✆ 62233, Open year round: 9-18. Various representatives of local wildlife, ranging from lynx to moufflon can be seen in open-air enclosures along a hiking trail. Tree nursery with more than 60 varieties of trees and shrubs.

🔲 **Waldschwimmbad (public pool)**, ✆ 61366, Open: May-early Sept, daily 9-20.

Records from the year 788 also show the existence of a settlement where Niederndorf today lies. The area was, however, first inhabited about 400 years before Christ, and the Romans built a road directly through the site. In 1704 many of the village's buildings were burned by the Bavarians during the war of the Spanish succession. Two years later, the Austrian Kaiser Josef I gave Niederndorf the right to hold an annual fair. In the following years the village prospered as a center for farriers, blacksmith and armourers. War returned to Niederndorf in the years after 1800, and bad weather caused several poor harvests in the years 1815 to 1817, but the town recovered until the deprivations of the 20th century's world wars. Since 1948 the town has experienced a lasting upswing with the construction of a public swimming pool, new schools, a

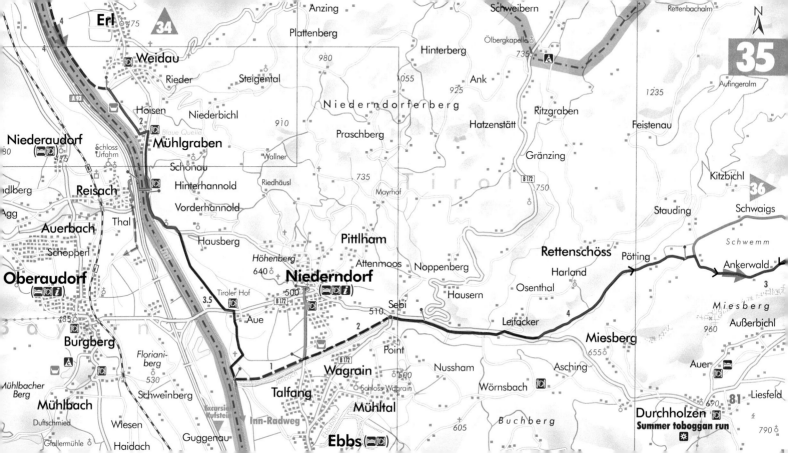

fire department and other infrastructure improvements. The population of about 2,500 residents have a wide range of recreational opportunities and associations, including a tennis club, a gymnastics club, orchard and garden associations and the village's own theatre, the "s'Theata Niederndorf."

Tip: Niederndorf makes a good starting point for an excursion to "the pearl of the Tyrol," the city of Kufstein. From Niederndorf simply follow the Inn Valley bicycle trail via the towns of Ebbs and Oberndorf.

Kufstein
Postal code: A-6330; Telephone area code: 05372
🛈 **Tourism association**, Unterer Stadtpl. 8, ☎ 62207
🚢 **Tyrol Inn schifffahrt (ship line)**. Departures from late April-Oct: 10:30-14, July/Aug 14 and 16 for a 2-hour cruise.
🏛 **Fortress museum**, Open: Closed mid-Nov to mid-Dec. Collection includes prehistoric artifacts and displays on farming, industry and zoology.
🏛 **Sewing machine museum**, Kinkstraße, Open: Mon-Sun. Museum in memory of Joseph Madersperger, in the house of his birth.
🏛 **Museum SINNFonie and Schauglasbläserei (glass making)**, Weißbachstraße
❸ **Kufstein castle**, dates to 1205, open air theatre.

❌ **Heldenorgel** in castle tower. Build in 1931, the largest free-standing organ in the world.
❌ **Wilder Kaiser chairlift**, Open: May-Oct 9-16.

The city of Kufstein grew at the foot of a commanding bluff surrounded by the steep slopes of the Kaiser and Thiersee ranges of mountains that form a gate between the Inn valley and the foothills of the Alps. This natural border made the town strategically important, and for hundreds of years it was a point of conflict between Tyrol and the rulers of Bavaria.

It also explains the importance of the castle that was first built around 1200 to help defend the location. Over the centuries the castle was constantly modernized and expanded to stay abreast of military advances. As a result Kufstein has a rich military history: when Kaiser Maximilian I captured the city in 1504, it was the first time artillery played a decisive role in the battle for a European city. The medieval character of the city suffered damage during the war of the Spanish succession, the Tyrolian war of independence, and aerial bombardment in 1944.

Niederndorf to Kranzach   11.5 km
Continue up the route along the Jennbach stream as far as the B 172 main road ～ continue straight at the intersection with the B 172 ～ turn right towards Sebi ～ take the pedestrian/bicycle path to the right of the road ～ ride gently uphill ～ and continue along the bike path ～ which crosses to the other side of the road and then turns left at a sawmill ～ follow the sign for "Radroute Richtung Walchsee" towards Pötting ～ turn left towards Walchsee/Rettenschöss ～ take the curve to the left over a bridge ～ and ride up the right side of a stream ～ and up the mountain to Pötting.

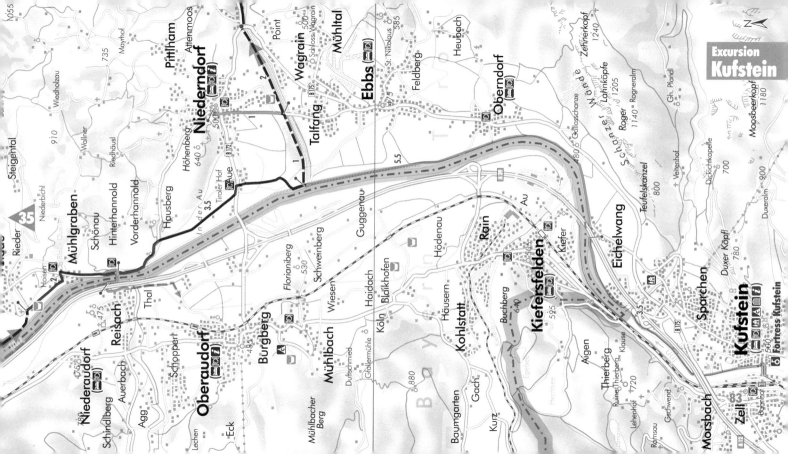

Steigental

Rieder

35

Niederbichl

Wiedholzau

910

735

Mayrhof

Wallner

Riedhäusl

Pittham

Attenmoos

Niederdorf

Höhenberg

640

500

Point

Wagrain

500

Schloss Wagrain

Mühltal

St. Nikolaus

585

Ebbs

Feldberg

Heubach

Oberndorf

Zehnerkopf

1240

Wände

Lahnköpfe

1205

Roger

1140

Rogneralm

Gh. Pfandl

Veitenhof

Dickichkapelle

700

Moosbeerkopf

1180

900

Duxeralm

Mühlgraben

Schönau

Hinterhannold

Vorderhannold

Hausberg

In der Au

Tiroler Hof

3.5

Aue

5.5

Guggenau

Florianiberg

Schweinberg

530

Hödenau

Au

Rain

Kiefer

Gallaschanze

Schanzer

Teufelskanzel

800

Eichelwang

780

Sparchen

Duxer Köpfl

Kufstein

500

🏰 Fortress Kufstein

Hoisen

Reisach

475

Thal

Schoppert

Burgberg

485

Mühlbach

Wiesen

Haidach

Köln

Blaikhofen

Häusern

Kohlstatt

Buchberg

640

Kiefersfelden

525

Aigen

Thierberg

Ruine Thierberg

720

Klause

Egerbach

Gföllermühle

Duftschmied

Duftschmied

880

Baumgarten

Gach

Kurz

Hechtsee

Lehenhof

Römsau

Gschwend

Morsbach

Bahnhof

Zell

83

Niederaudorf

475

Schindlberg

Auerbach

Agg

Lechen

Oberaudorf

Eck

Schoppert

Mühlbacher Berg

Talfang

1055

Pötting

Ride past the chapel and through the village ～ turn left at the junction, following the sign ～ then turn right, following the wooden sign towards Walchsee ～ stay left at the fork ～ and pass a small pond and continue uphill ～ through a farmyard ～ below to the left one can see the Schwemm bottomland ～ pass the gravel pit and ride downhill ～ and into the town of Walchsee ～ stay right at the intersection and continue along the side of the stream ～ stay on the bike path next to the stream and cross the B 172 ～ turn left just before the campground and cross the bridge and turn left again ～ and follow the curve to the right into Walchsee.

Walchsee

Postal code: A-6344; Telephone area code: 05374

🛈 **Tourism Information**, Dorfplatz 10, ☎ 52230

🕌 **St. Johannes parish church**

🛏 **Wittlinger Therapy center**, Alleestr. 30, ☎ 5245. Pools, whirlpool, massage, sauna and solarium.

🏨 **Hotel Seehof**, Kranzach 20, ☎ 5661

The village of Walchsee is a popular tourism center located on the banks of the Walchsee

Kranzach

lake. Visitors can take advantage of a wide range of sport and recreational facilities, including three public beaches. Other sports available include water skiing, windsurfing, sailing, fishing, tennis, biking and minigolf. There is also a summer toboggan run and facilities for kite flying and paragliding. The village is also interesting for nature-lovers. The nearby "Schwemm" is a bog formed by an Ice Age lake. The 63-hectare nature reserve is home to many rare and threatened species of plants and animals.

The route goes past the church and down to the public beach ～ stay to the left and then turn right on the main road ～ when you reach the edge of town take the bike path along the shore to Kranzach.

Tip: If one takes a left in Kranzach, towards Ried and Grundharting, one reaches a very pretty route to the interesting village of Kössen.

Kössen

Postal code: A-6345; Telephone area code: 05375

🛈 **Tourism association Kössen-Schwendt**, Info office, Dorf 15, ☎ 6287, www.koessen.at

🕌 **St. Peters parish church**, Dorf 8, ☎ 6244. The most imposing structure in the town and one of the most significant churches in the lower Tyrol. Earliest recorded mention dates from 1197. Rebuilt as late-gothic church in the 16th century. Current baroque structure dates from the early 18th century, and includes 14 stations of the cross by Simon Benedikt Faistenberger.

🕌 **"Maria Klobenstein" pilgrimage church. Church consisting of 3 chapels on a dramatic site off the road towards** Schleching. The name "Klobenstein" refers to the riven 18-meter boulder next to the church.

✳ **Kössen formations.** Geological formations of dark marl, black slate and dark limestone consisting of upper Triassic layers that contain large numbers of fossils. Especially accessible near the Loferbach, along the Bundesstraße to Reit im Winkl, just before the Austrian border, and near the Entenlochklamm.

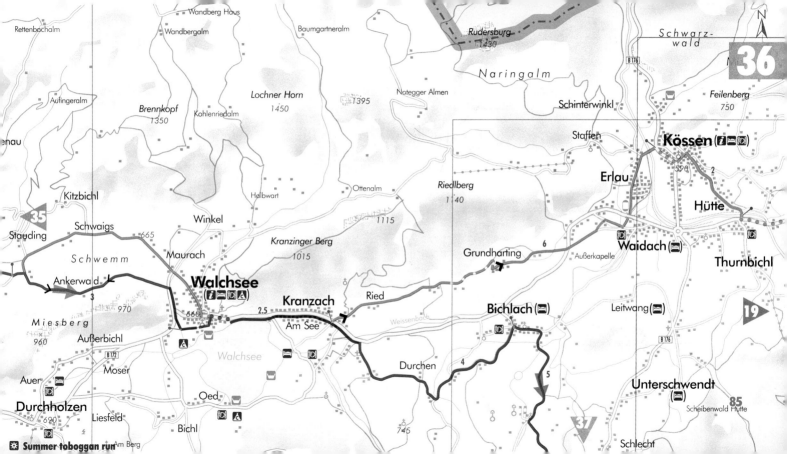

Rettenbachalm

Wandberg Haus

Wandbergalm

Baumgartneralm

Rudersburg
1430

Schwarz-
wald

Naringalm

36

Aufingeralm

Brennkopf
1350

Lochner Horn
1450

Kohlenriedalm

1395

Notegger Almen

Schinterwinkl

Feilenberg
750

Staffen

Kössen (i ⌂ ▣)

590

Kitzbichl

Halbwart

Ottenalm

Riedlberg
1140

Erlau

2

35

Schwaigs

665

Winkel

1115

Hütte

Stauding

Schwemm

Maurach

Kranzinger Berg
1015

Grundharting

6

Außerkapelle

Waidach (⌂)

Thurnbichl

Ankerwald

3

Walchsee
(i ▣ ▣ ⌂)

Ried

Leitwang (⌂)

19

970

660

2.5

Kranzach

Miesberg
960

Außerbichl

Am See

Weissenbach

Bichlach (⌂)

B 172

Walchsee

Durchen

4

Auer

Moser

Durchholzen
690

Oed

Liesfeld

Bichl

5

Unterschwendt
(⌂)

B 176

37

85

Scheibenwald Hütte

Am Berg

745

Schlecht

✳ **Summer toboggan run**

Kohlental

📧 **Erlebnis Waldbad** swimming and recreation complex, Schwimmbadweg, 📞 6287, Open: mid May- mid Sept, daily 9-19.
🚲 **Sporthotel Tyrol**, Dorf 12, 📞 6241

Kranzach to Griesenau   13 km
Kranzach
To stay on the main route ride out of Kranzach and cross the **Weißenbach** stream on the **B 176** ~ and turn right towards **Durchen**.
Durchen
Ride past a number of farmhouses ~ take the left towards Bichlach and Kössen.

Bichlach
In Bichlach turn right at the Hotel Riedl ~ and after just a few meters turn right again towards Schwendt ~ the village of Schwendt can be seen on the hillside across the valley.
Schwendt
Postal code: A-6345; Telephone area code: 05375
🛈 **Tourism association Kössen-Schwendt**, Infobüro, Dorf 15, 📞 6287
Follow the signs through the **Kohlental** to the **Gasthof Griesenau** ~ the road crosses the **Kohlenbach stream** repeatedly ~ at times along the edge of the forest or into the forest.

Tip: At the Gasthof Griesenau one can turn right and head up the wild and romantic Kaiserbach valley.
Griesenau

Griesenau to Lofer   28.5 km
Stay to the left on the main road at the inn and the chapel ~ ride through Griesenau ~ and then gently uphill into the forest ~ and follow the **B 176 to** Gasteig.
Gasteig
At the far end of the village there's a pedestrian/bicycle path on the left side ~ turn

Landscape near Atzlbach

left at the intersection towards Kirchdorf i. Tirol from Schwendter Straße onto **Gasteiger Straße** ~ and 1.5 kilometers down a steep and curvy road ~ a sharp curve to the right coming into the valley ~ past the house at **Unteranger No. 1** ~ take the pedestrian-bicycle path on the right into Kirchdorf.
Kirchdorf i. Tirol
Postal code: A-6382; Telephone area code: 05352
🛈 **Tourism association**, Litzlfeldner Str. 2, 📞 6933
🏛 **St. Stephan church**, Dorfplatz
✳ **Kirchdorf lake**, 📞 6933. Guided tours available for the hydro-electric dam at the lake.

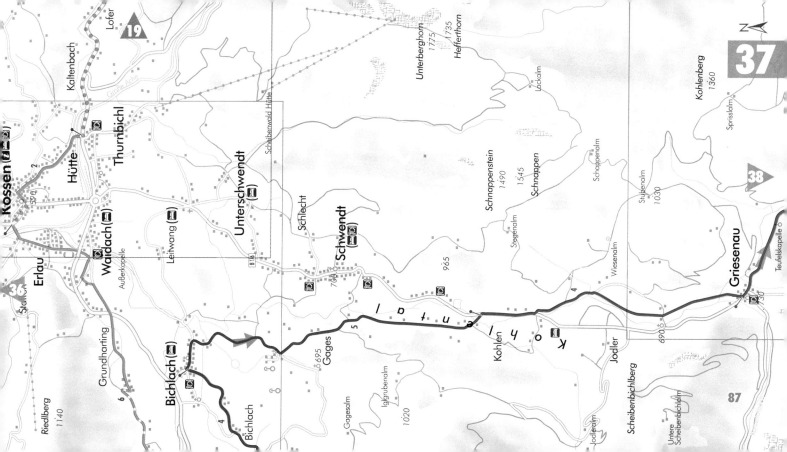

Lofer

19

Kaltenbach

Thurnbichl

Kössen

Hütte

2

590

Erlau

Station

36

Waidach

Außerkapelle

Grundharting

Riedlberg
1140

6

Leitwang

Bichlach

Bichlach

4

Unterschwendt

Scheibenwald Hütte

Schlecht

Schwendt

B 176

695
Gages

Gagesalm
1020

Iglgrubenalm

695

5

Kohlen

Klausbachtal

965

700

Jodleralm

Untere
Scheibenbichlalm

Scheibenbichlberg

Jodler

Unterberghorn

Heffterhorn
1735

Lockalm

Schnappenstein
1490

Schnappen
1545

Schoppenalm

Stegenalm

Wiesenalm

Stubenalm
1030

4

690

Griesenau

30

Teufelskapelle

38

Kohlenberg
1360

Sprisslalm

N

87

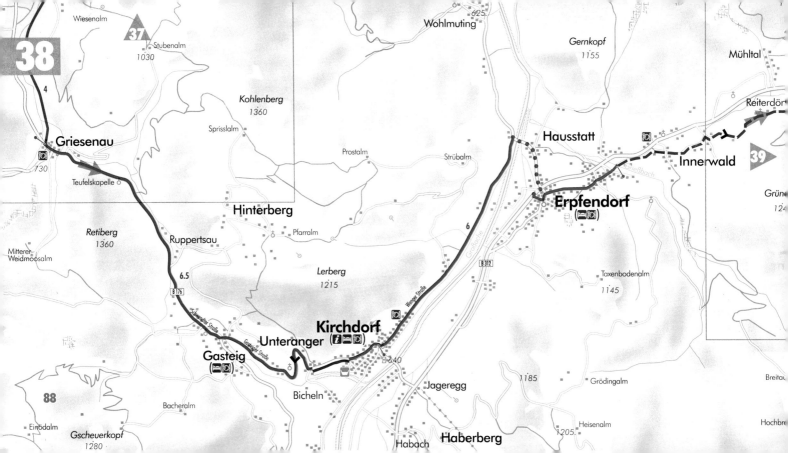

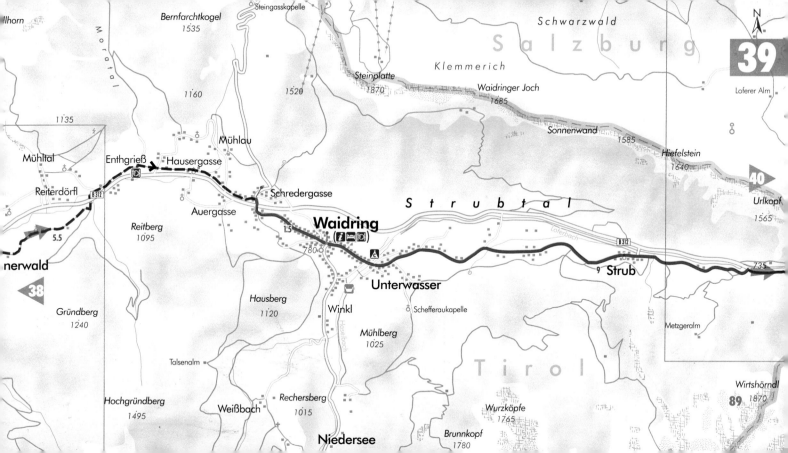

- ❄ **Metzgerhaus**, ✆ 6933. Historic farmhouse used for various events and exhibitions, plus guided tours by appointment.
- ⛰ **Grossache river adventure path**, ✆ 6933. Information plaques along the path provide information about the Kirchdorf flood prevention project
- ✉ **Outdoor pool**, Kaiserstr. 2, ✆ 66010, Open: mid May – mid Sept, daily 9-19.
- 🚲 **Schwabegger**, Dorfstr. 9, ✆ 63105

Ride into the town ∼ make the sharp right curve to the church ∼ and turn left at the church ∼ around the church and continue on **Wenger Straße** ∼ ride out of Kirchdorf along the stream parallel to the embankment along the Großache stream ∼ follow the road until the stream converges with the Großache ∼ turn right at the main road ∼ cross the bridge over the Großache and proceed to the Bundesstraße ∼ first turn right towards Innsbruck and then take the first left towards Erpfendorf.

Erpfendorf

Ride past the tourism information office and the church ∼ through a curve to the left and then take the next right turn ∼ pass the tennis courts ∼ ride out of Erpfendorf gently uphill along the edge of the forest ∼ cross the Gries-

bach stream ∼ and follow the bicycle route sign towards Waidring on an unpaved track ∼ cross a wooden bridge ∼ parallel to the Bundesstraße ∼ take a right across the stream and proceed along the right side of the stream ∼ at **Lärchenhof** the path is named **Rudersberg** and is unpaved as it follows the stream ∼ it gradually approaches the road ∼ directly next to the road cross a wooden bridge and then to the left under the road and then proceed on the other side.

Continue along the stream past the **Gasthaus Enthgrieß** ∼ the track has a gravel surface and returns to the road ∼ and goes uphill ∼ before going back down to the road ∼ cross a wooden bridge and to the left behind some houses parallel to the road ∼ past the Holzknechtstüberl restaurant and then to the left on the road before heading straight into Waidring.

Waidring

Postal code: A-6384; Telephone area code: 05353
- ℹ **Tourism association Waidring**, Dorfstr. 12, ✆ 5242
- 🏛 **Schäferau chapel**, prayer chapel located in the woods. "May devotions" are held here yearly. The interior features a copy of a Turkish Madonna.

- 🏛 **Village church**, Open: daily 7:30-18. Noteworthy baroque frescoes and interesting interior design.
- 🏛 **Lugmair bell foundry**, Dorfstr. 43, ✆ 5530, Guided tours early June – late September, Tues 10, Thurs 16 or by appointment.
- ❄ **Andrä Schreder wood carving shop**, Unterwasser 38, ✆ 5441, Open: Mon-Fri 10-12 and 14-18. Christmas crèches, wooden figures etc.
- 🚲 **Intersport Kienpointner**, Dorfstr. 6, ✆ 5451

Wolfgang Amadeus Mozart and his father passed through Waidring on August 13, 1771 in the course of his second Italy trip.

Take the main street through Waidring ∼ ride out of the village and stay on the road ∼ in the curve to the left go straight following the bicycle route sign to Lofer ∼ in the industrial zone of Waiding the route passes a bicyclists' rest area ∼ the route then goes into the forest and over a wooden bridge ∼ at the inn the road curves to the left ∼ take the paved local-traffic road that runs parallel to the main road ∼ go around a gate ∼ the bicycle route gets closer to the main road and then crosses the ⚠ heavily-traveled road ∼ take the narrow path that runs downhill along the Loferbach stream ∼ proceed on the left side of the stream parallel to the road ∼

under one bridge and then immediately under another bridge.

Take the paved path over a wooden bridge and under a third bridge ~ the bicycle path arrives in Lofer at a brown wooden house ~ go straight over the bridge and turn left on the street ~ pass the playing fields to the left of the street ~ turn left directly in front of the **Salzburgerhof** and ride into the center of Lofer.

Lofer

Postal code: A-5090; Telephone area code: 06588

🛈 Tourism association Sbg. Saalachtal, Lofer 310, ✆ 83210

🅰 **Prax Eishöhle**, ✆ 519 or 520. A tunnel cave formed mainly during the tertiary period and the following ice ages. Guided tours available (7 to 9 hours, 2 hours in the caves). Minimum age 15. Appropriate shoes and clothing required.

✖ **Kajak & Rafting Fun**, Motion Center Andreas Vogelstätter, ✆ 7524

Early in its history Lofer was an important post station, which brought innkeepers and blacksmiths to the village. Traders and other craftsmen followed, and in 1232 the town gained the status of market. Lofer prospered over the centuries, until construction of the Gisela railroad from Salzburg to Innsbruck. It went through Zell

Mountain panorama near Bad Reichenhall

am See and Saalfelden, and took with it much of Lofer's economic activity. Townspeople soon discovered the potential in attracting visitors to the area and established Lofer's first tourism association in 1883. A pool was built in 1892, followed in 1900 by the first tennis courts. Bus service between Lofer and Bad Reichenhall began in 1910. Today Lofer remains a popular vacation destination in summer as well as winter.

On December 13, 1769 Wolfgang Amadeus Mozart and his father departed Salzburg on their way to Italy. About 7 p.m. that evening they arrived in Lofer and spent the night at the home of Johann Chrysostomus Helmreich. On the same

day, Christian Fürchtegott Gellert, the noted German poet who corresponded with Mozart's father, died in Leipzig. Mozart mentions Gellert's death a month later in a letter to his sister. On December 14, Mozart and his father departed Lofer, arriving in Wörgl that evening.

Lofer to Bad Reichenhall   25.5 km

After riding through Lofer return to the main Bundestraße to the left ~ at the first opportunity turn right ~ the quiet track is paved only in parts as it follows the course of the Saalach towards Unken ~ the track ends at the village of Reit, just before Unken ~ take the bicycle path to **Kniepass** ~ cross the Unkenbach stream at the **Lukaswirt inn** and take Dorfstraße through the village to the Steinpass.

Unken

Postal code: A-5091; Telephone area code: 06589

🛈 Information spot, ✆ 4202

🏛 Kalkofengut local history house, ✆ 4502, Open: 15 June-15 Sept, Tues- Sun in the afternoons. Exhibits about farm living, local crafts and artifacts from the Bronze and Hallstatt periods.

✉ Recreation center, ✆ 4300. Indoor pool, sauna, outdoor pool and giant water slide, whirlpool and much more.

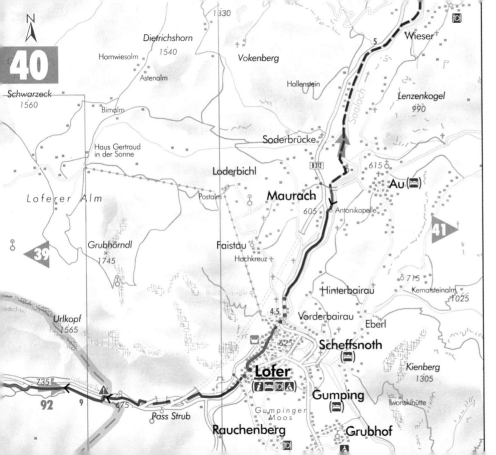

The origin of the name Unken remains unclear to this day. Throughout history the village crops up repeatedly with numerous variations on the name: Unchine, Vnchen, Uncna, Vunchne or Hunche. The earliest recorded mention of Unken dates to the year 1137, when Provost Gerhoch von Reichersberg transferred ownership of a salt mine near Unken. Reichersberg, incidentally, lies near the Inn river in upper Austria on the route of the Tauern bicycle trail. Unken today is a popular destination in summer and winter, with a wide variety of activities available for visitors, including cross country skiing, ski tours, curling, hiking, biking and a recreation center.

Just before the customs offices on the **Steinpass** turn right town to the Saalach and then cross the river ∾ the Saalach here forms the border between Germany and Austria ∾ ride this quiet path through the beautiful landscape along the "green frontier" ∾ the border is a wooden fence which can be crossed on a small bridge.

Having crossed into Bavaria, ride up a short hill ∾ continue through the forest ∾ past the old bridge at Schneizlreuth and along the right bank of the river.

Two more kilometers of up and down terrain take the trail to the main road at **Unterjettenberg** ∾ stay to the left ∾ cross the Saalach on the old stone bridge and then turn right ∾ through the village of Fronau and

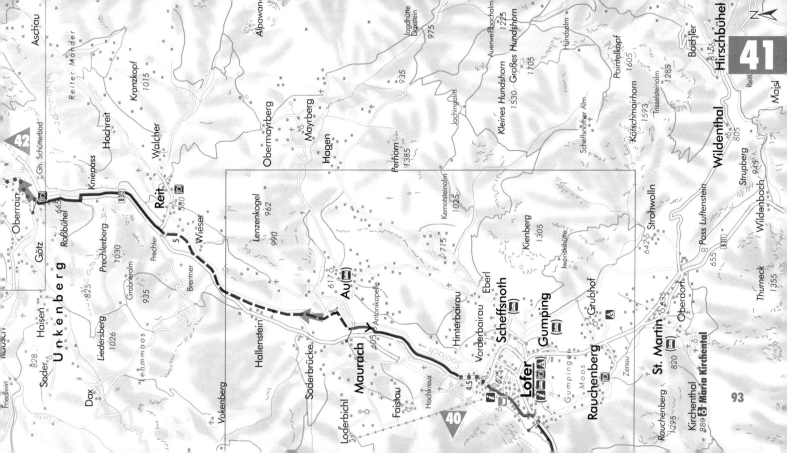

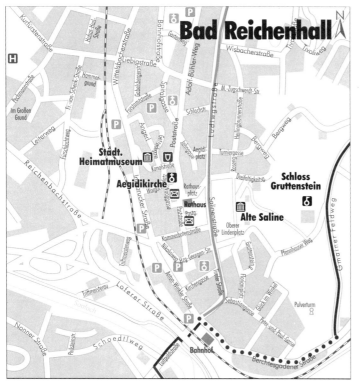

Bad Reichenhall

proceed down the pretty forest trail along the Saalach reservoir ~ soon the trail enters the edges of Bad Reichenhall and passes the ground-station of the famous **Predigtstuhlbahn cable car** and onto **Thumseestraße** ~ turn right across the **Luitpold bridge** ~ take the underpass beneath **Loferer Straße** to reach the old center of Bad Reichenhall.

Bad Reichenhall

Postal code: D-83435; Telephone area code: 08651

- 🛈 **Resort and Tourism association** e.V., Wittelsbacher Str. 15, ✆ 606-303
- 🏛 **City history museum**, Getreideg. 4, ✆66821, Open: May-Oct, Tues-Fri 14-18 and every 1st Sunday from 10-12. Museum about the settlement of the Saalach valley and development of salt mining.
- 🏛 **Salt museum** in der Alten Saline, ✆ 7002146, Open: April-Oct, daily 10-11:30 and 14-16; Nov-March, Tues/Thurs 14-16. Museum about Reichenhall salt, well-

digging and the history of salt-mining techniques. Guided tours available.

- 🏰 **St. Zeno church**
- 🏰 **Aegidi church**, Aegidipl. Church built in 1159
- 🏰 **Burg Gruttenstein** with historic city wall towers over the Alte Saline. Today the castle is privately owned.
- ✱ **Aegidiplatz** with Alte Feuerhaus (old firehouse, today a continuing-education school), a gallery, the city music school and a cabaret.
- ✱ **Alte Rathaus** on the Rathausplatz, built 1849 and decorated with frescoes in 1924.
- ✱ **Open air salt vapors inhalation center** is located in the health spa.
- 🛁 **Rupertus baths**, Open: Mon 13:30-19:30, Tues-Sun 8:30-19:30. Therapeutic salt-water spa and outdoor pool.
- 🛁 **City pool**, Open: Mon-Fri 14-21:30; Sat, Sun, Hol 10-21:30

The city of Bad Reichenhall is marvelously situated in a valley in Bavaria's Berchtesgadener land. From the beginning it was salt – at one time referred to as "white

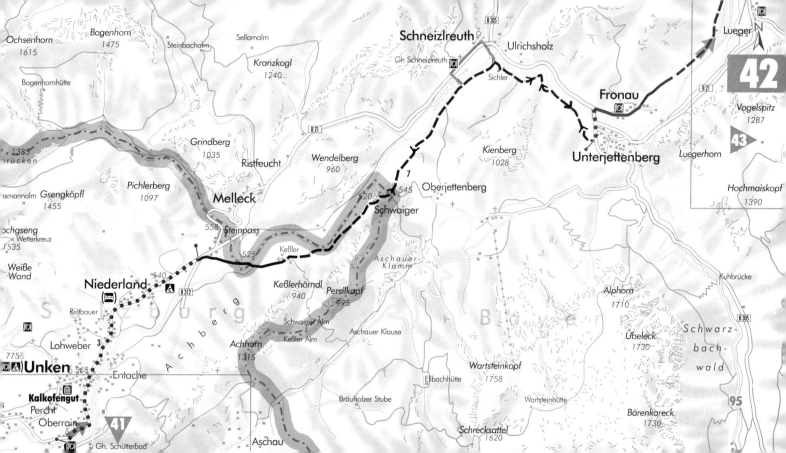

gold" – that shaped the city's history and made Bad Reichenhall famous across Europe. The Salt Museum in the Alte Saline shows how salt was mined in the past and today.

The picturesque mountains that surround the city and the Mediterranean ambience of the old town make Bad Reichenhall especially attractive to visitors. The city also has a great deal to offer, be it comfortable cafés and restaurants or facilities for sports and medical therapy to cultural events.

Tip: There are two different routes for reaching Salzburg by bicycle from Bad Reichenhall. The shorter variant runs through the Saalach valley, and an alternative leads through Berchtesgaden and Hellbrunn. The Saalach valley route follows the Tauern Radweg.

The Saalach Valley   *21.5 km*

After the underpass go uphill and make a sharp right turn ~ and to the left into the old town – **Tiroler Straße** ~ dismount and push your bicycle through the pedestrian zone ~ Tiroler Straße then becomes **Salinenstraße,** after which it is named **Ludwigsstraße,** and

Castle near Marzoll

finally **Salzburger Straße** ~ the pedestrian zone ends at Kurgarten and you may remount your bicycle on **Salzburger Straße** ~ follow the bicycle route sign towards Marzoll/St. Zeno ~ in quick succession pass the **St. Zeno** church and cemetery ~ turn right on **Marzoller Weg** ~ this street makes a tight curve to the right and then to the left into **Froschhamer Weg** cul-de-sac ~ ride down the hill and on a short piece of paved road ~ then go right on the unpaved track ~ past the lumber yard and back onto an asphalt street ~ parallel with the main Bundesstraße gently downhill ~ over a small wooden bridge

~ the track is narrow ~ turn right when you come to the larger road and continue straight ahead.

Weißbach

The route runs through flat terrain between Weißbach and Marzoll ~ take **Grenzlandstraße to** Marzoll.

Marzoll

To the right there is a palace ~ the route goes past the palace, a hotel and then a church ~ after the last houses the route becomes a farm service track ~ cross the border between Bavaria and Austria ~ take the asphalt road to the left and then turn left on the larger right-of-way road ~ use the pedestrian/bicycle path on the right ~ and follow the signs for the Tauern Radweg bicycle route.

Tip: Here one can turn right for a side-trip to the Salzburg outdoor museum. It is open from March 22 to November 2 and December 26 to January 6, Tuesday to Sundays from 9-18 o'clock.

The bicycle route runs next to the road ~ arrive in **Wartberg** ~ and pass the Gasthaus Wartberg ~ the bicycle path ends and the route

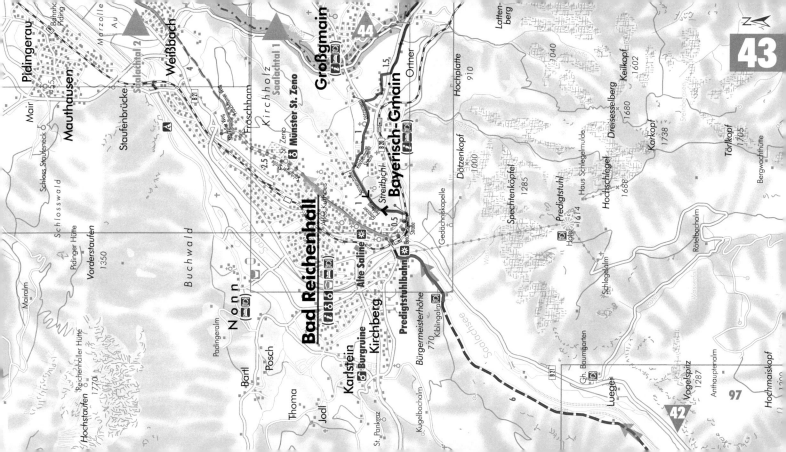

Leopoldskron castle

continues on the road ~ turn right just before the Autobahn ~ on a paved road ~ after a short distance turn left on the field track ~ the route passes close to the Autobahn ~ crosses a small bridge and curves to the left.

Tip: Note the fine views of the mountains around Salzburg!

Take the curve to the left on the cobble-stone road underneath the Autobahn ~ the road surface here is very rough.

Gois

Turn to the right on **Salzweg** ~ go straight on the main road ~ stay on **Goiser Straße** past the stables ~ and leave Gois ~ turn right on the main road ~ ride under the Autobahn and take **Viehhauser Straße** to Viehhausen ~ turn right on **Laschenskystraße** and ride out of Viehhausen ~ next comes **Viehhausen-Laschensky** ~ curve to the left through the **Schweizersiedlung** ~ turn right on Waldstraße towards Glansiedlung.

Glansiedlung

Take the main road straight across the bridge ~ and immediately turn left on the bicycle path ~ and proceed along the Glanbach stream ~ and turn right on **Schwarzgraben-weg** ~ take **Birkenallee** to **Moosstraße** and turn left ~ onto the pedestrian/bicycle path ~ then turn right on **Josef Moosbrucker Weg** ~ which soon becomes **Georg Nikolaus von Nissen Straße** ~ follow the signs to the left to **König Ludwig Straße** ~ ride along the edge of the Leopoldskroner pond with the fine views of the Leopoldskron palace and the **Hohensalzburg fortress** ~ the bike path ends on **Firmianstraße** where the route turns right ~ turn right on **Leopoldskroner Allee** ~ use the pedestrian/bicycle path on the left

44 **Bad Reichenhall**
(i)(🛏)(🍴) ▭ ⛽

Alte Saline ✿

Großgmain
(i)(🍴) ▭

43

Streitbühl
Bayerisch-Gmain
(i) ▭ ▭

✿ Berchtesgadener Straße
Predigtstuhlbahn

Ortner

Gedächniskapelle

Dötzenkopf
1000

Hochplatte
910

45

Spechtenköpfel

Pass Hallthurm

Münster St. Zeno
St. Zeno

Ruine Plain
635

B 21 · B 20 · B 21 · B 20

and bear right towards the center of Salzburg ~ curve to the left towards Anif ~ the bicycle path crosses the street and goes straight to the **Sinnhubstraße** ~ cross Sinnhubstraße and then turn left along Sinnhubstraße ~ turn left at the intersection with the traffic signal ~ continue on the bicycle path next to **Fürste-**

nallee ~ through the curve and then turn left on **Erzabt Klotz Straße** ~ which empties into **Petersbrunnstraße** ~ which you take to **Nonntaler bridge** ~ where the alternate route rejoins the main route ~ turn to page 106 to continue the route.

Bad Reichenhall to Berchtesgaden   20 km

In Bad Reichenhall after the tunnel under the railroad go uphill to the right and then turn right ~ pass the filling station ~ take the bicycle path on the left side.

Tip: From Bad Reichenhall to Berchtesgaden the Mozart Bike Trail follows the route taken by the Bodensee-Königssee (Lake Constance–Königssee) Bicycle Trail. More information about this 414 kilometer route along the southern edge of Bavaria can be found in the *bikeline* **Bodensee-Königssee Radtourenbuch** (available in German).

After 500 meters turn left on **Gmainer Feldweg** and go up the steep hill ~ pass to the right of a palace ~ and go straight on the bicycle path which ends after several hundred meters ~ continue gently downhill on **Sonnenstraße**.

Bayerisch Gmain
Postal code: D-83457; Telephone area code: 08651
🛈 Tourist Info, Großgmainer Str. 14, ✆ 606401

From **Sonnenstraße** turn right on **Reichenhaller Straße** and proceed straight ～ at the fork bear to the left following the main street ～ pass to the right of the **Bayerisch Gmain church** at the next junction turn left on **Dötzenweg**.

Cross **Großgmainer Straße** ～ gently downhill ～ left along the **Kurgarten** ～ and continue on **Dorfbauernstraße** ～ left on **Untersbergstraße** and down to the **B 20 main road** cross to the other side and take the pedestrian/bicycle path that runs along the B 20 to **Römerstraße** ～ then continue on **Hohenfriedstraße** ～ through the tunnel ～ past the playing fields ～ and then continue on the bicycle path on the left side of the road.

After about 1.5 kilometers the bicycle path turns left into the forest ～ uphill through the woods in a south-easterly direction ～ after one kilometer return to the asphalt bicycle path on the left side of the B 20 ～ it ends after another 500 meters ～ turn left on the gravel track towards Hallthurm.

Hallthurm

Take **Reichenhaller Straße** through the village ～ a short stretch on an asphalt cul-de-sac

～ at the fork take the unpaved farm track through the woods.

Pass several benches ～ to the right there is a game enclosure ～ turn right at the next junction ～ and follow the course of the road towards the right ～ to the left note the **Hof Holzstube** ～ turn right on **Holzstubenweg** at the junction.

At the first houses the asphalt resumes ～ turn right at the T-intersection ～ cross the railroad tracks ～ turn left on the B 20 and ride a short distance on the moderately busy road ～ cross a bridge ～ use the bicycle path on the right side of the B 20.

The railroad is to the left ～ cross another bridge ～ the bicycle path switches to the other side of the road ～ and runs parallel to the road as it passes a filling station ～ through curves as it descends gently downhill ～ the path stays to the right of the village of **Winkl** and a playing field ～ and goes under a bridge.

Bischofswiesen

Postal code: D-83483; Telephone area code: 08652

i **Tourism office**, Hauptstr. 40, ✆ 977220

Tip: As an alternative to the main Mozart Bike Trail one can stay on the bicycle trail that

runs along the main road, the Staatsstraße (the orange route). It is relatively flat all they way to Berchtesgaden.

At the church in Bischofswiesen go to the right ~ ride through the village ~ at the traffic light turn left onto **Aschauerweiherstraße** ~ the road is fairly steep uphill and goes through several curves ~ stay on the Aschauerweiherstraße at the fork with Am Rostwald.

Tip: If you turn right at this fork, the road goes through Rostwald to Berchtesgaden directly to the Königliches Schloss.

Pass the parking lot to the left of the "Naturbad Aschauerweiher, Wander- and Langlaufzentrum" (Aschauerweiher hiking and cross-country center) ~ and then straight ahead ~ turn left onto Locksteinstraße at the intersection with Gerner Straße ~ follow the street down a steep section which ends at "Nonntal" ~ this street leads directly to the **Königliches Schloss Berchtesgaden.**

Berchtesgaden
Postal code: D-83471; Tel. area code: 08652

🅸 **Berchtesgaden Tourismus GmbH**, Königseer Str. 2, ✆ 9670

🅸 **Tourism office**, Maximilianstr. 9, ✆ 9445300

🅸 **Verkehrsbüro Oberau**, Roßfeldstr. 22, ✆ 964960

🏛 **Schloss Adelsheim local history museum**, Schroffenbergallee 6, ✆ 4410, Open: year-round, Mon-Fri 10-15. Collection of local art and culture, wood carvings, traditional costumes, furniture.

🏛 **Dokumentation Obersalzberg**, Salzbergstr. 41, ✆ 947960, Open: May-Oct, Tues-Sun 9-17; Nov-March, Tues-Sun 10-15. Multi-media exhibition about how the Nazi leadership used the village of Obersalzberg between 1933 and 1945.

🏛 **Salzbergwerk (salt mine)**, ✆ 60020, Open: May-mid October and Easter, daily 9-17; mid Oct-April, Mon-Fri 12:30-15:30; Rafting trip across the Salt lake, film presentation, 1-hour guided tour in which visitors put on traditional miners clothes and enter the mine in a mining wagon.

🅱 **Königliches Schloss**, Schlosspl. 2, ✆ 947980, Open: year-round. Art collection includes paintings, sculptures, furniture, tapestries and Nymphenburg porcelain from the 15th to 19th centuries.

✳ The historic center of Berchtesgaden has numerous noteworthy old houses and picturesque squares.

✳ The 2713-meter **Watzmann** mountain is the town's best-known landmark.

✳ Excellent views of the land around Berchtesgaden can be had from the **Kehlsteinhaus** (Eagle's nest). Elevator open May-Oct, Infos available at ✆ 967-0.

🅰 **National park Berchtesgadener Land**. Infos available from National park house Berchtesgaden, Franziskuspl. 7, ✆ 64363, Open: daily 9-17. Exhibits about Alpine environment. Videos, slideshows

Berchtesgaden

🛁 **Watzmann Therme baths**, Bergwerkstr. 54, ✆ 94640. Interesting spa with slides, steam baths, sauna, solarium and pools.

Bavarian royalty made the Konigliches Schloss in Berchtesgaden one of their favorite summer retreats. The Watzmann mountain towers majestically over the town, with its dramatic eastern face dropping precipitously into the glittering Königssee. As in Bad Reichenhall, salt played an important role in the Berchtesgaden's growth. Salt water was also used by the city's spas, which diluted the brine and applied it in therapies for skin conditions and other ailments. The entire spa area and Berchtesgadener Land nature preserve were designated a UNESCO Berchtesgaden biosphere reserve in 1990.

46

Winkl

Rauhenkopf
1605

Almbachklamm ✱

Oberstein

47

Oberau

Hintergern

Brändelberg
935

Lercheck

Obergern

Kneifelspitze
1190

Reckensberg
535

Pauls-Hütte

Vordergern

Bischofswiesen

Unterau

1030

Berchtesgadener
Bürgerwald

Metzenleiten

Untersalzberg I

Anzenbach

Laros

Salt mine

Rostwald

Königliches Schloss

Sillberg

Stanggass

Böcklmühle

Bader

Berchtesgaden

Obersalzberg

Buchhöhe

Klingeckkogel
1140

Strub

Untersalzberg II

Oberschönau I

Mitterbach

Schwarzort

Berchtesgaden

Heimatmuseum - Schloss Adelsheim

Salt mine

Lockstein

Kälberstein

Watzmann-therme

Rathaus Rathaus-platz Schloss-platz

Königliches Schloss

Oberkälberstein

Kur-garten

Salzbergstraße

Solekurbad

Hauptbahnhof

Kurklinik

Ramsauer Str.

Salzberg Cable Car

Bodensee-Königssee-Radweg

Berchtesgaden to Salzburg   28 km

Take **Maximilianstraße** downhill to **Bahnhofstraße** ~ turn left towards Salzburg ~ cross the first intersection and at the second intersection turn right on **Bergwerksstraße** towards the Eisstadion (ice stadium) ~ cross the iron bridge across the **Berchtesgadener Ache** ~ pass playing fields ~ the river is to the left ~ pass the **Berchtesgaden salt mine** ~ turn right on Wiesenweg before you reach the bridge ~ the bicycle route now runs along the side of the Berchtesgadener Ache ~ the track is not paved until the next bridge, where asphalt resumes ~ stay on the narrow track past several farms ~ the track returns to the B 305 main road ~ before reaching the road stay left and go under the bridge ~ to the other side of the road where there is a bicycle path towards **Unterau** ~ staying on the right side of the river.

Before the road curves to the left the bicycle path crosses the Berchtesgadener Ache ~ and continues on the other bank ~ follow the bicycle route signs towards Marktschellenberg ~ about 100 meters after the bridge turn left on the unpaved track ~ along the river ~ on the gravel path to the **Kugelmühle** inn ~ cross the parking lot and take the wooden bridge ~ following the paved trail ~ then proceed on the Alte Deutsche Alpenstraße ~ and ride along the **Alte Berchtesgadener Straße** through the village ~ downhill towards **Marktschellenberg** ~ through a curve to the right and then turn left ~ and simply follow the main street through the village.

Marktschellenberg

Postal code: D-83487; Telephone area code: 08650

ℹ Tourism office, Salzburger Str. 2, ☎ 988830

✿ Schellenberger ice cave, ☎ 988830, Open: Whitsun – early Oct, daily 10-16, guided tours start every hour. The Schellenberger ice cave is the only ice cave in Germany that can be entered. The tour provides information about the formation of caves and ice caves.

The earliest recorded mention of Marktschellenberg dates to the year 1112. Like other old communities in the region, it long prospered from the salt mines. When salt production and the town's economic fortunes started to decline, the population turned to other industries, including the production of salt-bags, knitting, basket weaving and the clay production. Most of these enterprises did not last long, but Marktschellenberg eventually regained its economic base, thanks in part to the production of marbles made from Untersberger marble. A growing tourism business also helped the town.

In recent years Marktschellenberg has gained a reputation as a health resort town. There are hay and whey baths, Kneipp therapy institutes where Kneipp cures, saunas and solariums are available. The town also hosts the annual Marktschellenberg health weeks in March, where participants fast and cleanse their bodies under medical supervision. There are also a wide variety of health-oriented programs and events.

Depart Marktschellenberg in the direction of Grödig ~ the Königsseeache stream is to the right ~ the road descends gently through many curves ~ and soon crosses the border from Germany into Austria.

Hangendenstein

Starting from the border there is a paved bicycle path on the left side of the road ~ turn left at the traffic signal towards Grödig ~ the church in St. Leonhard is to the right, the tourism office is to the left.

St. Leonhard

Ride past the Hotel Untersberg ~ take the bicycle path on the left towards Grödig ~ the bicycle path ends at a bus stop.

Grödig

Postal code: D-5082; Telephone area code: 06246

ℹ Town office, Dr.-Richard-Hartmann-Str. 1, ☎ 72106-0

ℹ Tourism association, Gartenauerstr. 8, ☎ 73570

▣ Radio museum, Hauptstr. 3, ☎ 72857, Open: Weds 15-19 or by appointment. Subject: history and development of radio.

▣ Untersberger marble museum, ☎ 76411 or ☎ 74096, Open: May-Oct, Sat, Sun, Hol 13-18, Nov-April, Sat, Sun, Hol 13-17. Museum about the history of Unterberg marble.

Cross a bridge and ride through the quaint town ~ turn right on **Schützenstraße** in front of the church ~ along the cemetery and past a restaurant ~ under the Autobahn ~ and then immediately left onto **Eichetmühlweg** ~ at the fork stay right on **Sallwastlweg** ~ through a curve to the left and under the high-tension wires ~ turn right at the T-intersection at the edge of the woods ~ the asphalt surface ends at the first houses ~ after the woods turn left at the intersection ~ back onto asphalt surface ~ curve to the right and head straight for the **Zaunerhof** ~ after the farm turn right onto the private track ~ and head straight on **Herbert von Karajan Straße to** Anif.

Anif

Postal code: D-5081; Telephone area code: 06246

ℹ Tourism association, Fürstenweg 1, ☎ 72365

▣ Schloss Anif. The neo-gothic water palace is privately owned and not open to the public.

8 **Parish church**. Burial place of the conductor Herbert von Karajan.

Waldbad Anif, Open: May-Oct

Anif is also first mentioned in a document dating from 788. The castle Schloss Anif is known to have existed by the 16th century, though its foundations probably date to the middle of the 13th century. In 1530 ownership of the castle passed to the Salzburg Chancellor Niclas Ribeisen zu Leibgeding. After his death the castle passed from owner to owner until Count Alois von Arco-Steppberg claimed the property in 1837. He expanded and renovated the castle in the Romantic style, and completely refurbished many of the interior spaces. Today the castle is privately owned and not open

Salzburg and the Salzach River

to the public. The grounds are, however, opened twice a year: on the Feast of Corpus Christi, when church processions pass through the property, and on December 8 for the "Turmblasen" celebration during which Christmas carols are sung and schnapps, mulled wine and Christmas baked goods are consumed.

Turn left on **Brunnhausstraße** ∼ and right on **Halleiner Straße** ∼ turn left on **Mühleistraße across from the** Hotel Friesacher ∼ at the junction head uphill, following the sign for the "Tauern Radweg" ∼ pass the Hellbrunn zoo and through the extensive park until you reach **Fürstenweg** ∼ which leads straight to the palace **Schloss Hellbrunn**.

Tip: The palace with its famous water works and zoo is a few meters away.

Leave the palace grounds ∼ over the parking lot and follow the bicycle route sign towards the center of town ∼ along another avenue, the

Mozart bust on the Kapuzinerberg

Hellbrunner Allee ∼ past a number of smaller palaces.

The first of these palaces is Schloss Emsburg. It was built in 1618 and is not open to the public. A short distance further one passes Schloss Frohnburg, followed by Schloss Herrnau.

After Schloss Herrnau take **Hofhaymer Allee** and then **Freisaalweg** straight ahead.

To the right behind the hedges one can see Schloss Freisaal, a moated castle dating from 1549. The crowning finale to this "tour of the castles" is the Hohensalzburg castle.

Freisaalweg empties into **Akademiestraße** ∼ where you turn left ∼ cross **Erzabt Klotz Straße** onto **Zugallistraße** ∼ proceed on **Nonntaler Hauptstraße** ∼ before the courthouse turn left on **Kaigasse** and ride through the pedestrian zone to **Mozartsteg** ∼ follow the Salzach ∼ to the **Makartsteg** and then proceed on the other bank ∼ along

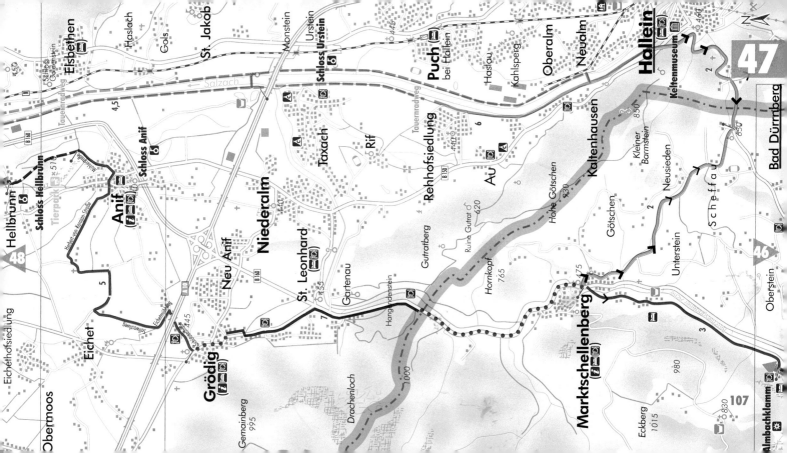

Hallein

Bad Dürrnberg

Keltenmuseum

Kaltenhausen

Kleiner Barmstein 850

Neusieden

Scheffau

Oberstein

Götschen

Unterstein

Marktschellenberg 475

Eckberg 1015

980

Almbachklamm

107

46

Hohe Götschen 830

Hornkopf 765

Ruine Gutrat 620

Gutratberg

1000

Drachenloch

Hangendenstein

Gartenau

St. Leonhard

Niederalm

Neu Anif

Grödig

Gemainberg 995

Eichet

Eichethofsiedlung

Obermoos

48

Hellbrunn

Schloss Hellbrunn

Tierpark

Anif

Schloss Anif

B160

Salzach

Tauernradweg

Elsbethen

Haslach

Gols

St. Jakob

Monstein

Urstein

Schloss Urstein

Puch bei Hallein

Haslau

Kahlsperg

Oberalm

Neualm

Toxach

Rif

Rehhofsiedlung

Au

B159

Tauernradweg

Schloss Goldenstein

450

4,5

5

445

6

Oberalm

Salzburg
48
Gnigl
1
Kühberg
710
Schloss Neuhaus
Haus der Natur
Schloss Mirabell
2.5
635
Kapuzinerberg
Mozart's birthplace
Parsch
Maxglan
Dom
Fortress Hohensalzburg
510
Gaisberg
Aigen
Abfalter
Schloss Leopoldskron
Saalachtal 2
Nonntal
Freisaalweg
Schloss Freisaal
3.5
Schloss Aigen
425
Leopoldskron
Kleingmain
endlersiedlung
4.5
Tauernradweg
Schloss Herrnau
425
4.5 Untermoos
435
4
Schloss Frohnburg
Glas
435
Gneis
Glansiedlung
Morzg
Schloss Emsburg
Hellbrunner Allee
Vorderfager
435
Glasenbach
Mittermoos
1.5
108
Hellbrunn
Eichethofsiedlung
Schloss Hellbrunn
450
47
B 150
Hengstberg
780
Obermoos
Schloss Goldenstein

Salzburger Dom

the quay to **Jahnstraße** where you turn right directly to the main train station.

Salzburg **go to page 12**

Bett & Bike

All hotels and inns in Germany that carry the Bett&Bike logo (♿) are bicycle-friendly businesses and members of the "Bed and Bike" project organized by the ADFC, Germany's largest bicycle riders' association. These businesses meet ADFC minimum requirements and offer special facilities for bicycle tourists.

Additional information about Bett&Bike locations can be found in the Bett&Bike listings available wherever *bikeline* bicycle tour-guides are sold.

Accommodations

The following list includes hotels (H, Hg, Hh), guest houses (Gh, P), farm houses (Bh) and rooms in private homes (Pz, BB = Bed&Breakfast), as well as youth hostels 🏠 and camp grounds ⛺ in most of the towns along the Mozart Bike Trail. Accommodations are listed by town in the order that those communities appear in the route descriptions.

This list does not claim to be complete and does not represent any kind of recommendation from the editors. The most important criteria for businesses listed here are proximity to the route and the centers of the main towns along the route.

The Roman numeral (I-VI) after the telephone number indicates the price classification of the lodgings. The key to prices is as follows:

I less than € 15
II €15 to € 23

III € 23 to € 30
IV € 30 to € 35
V € 35 to € 50
VI more than € 50

These ratings always refer to the price for a single person in a double with shower or bath and breakfast included. Rooms without private shower/bath are indicated by the symbol ⚠ after the price category.

We try to update this list constantly and welcome suggestions for new additions. Businesses listed here do not pay a fee for the listing.

Salzburg

Postal code: 5020; Tel. area code: 0662
🛈 Salzburg Information, Auerspergstr. 6, ✆ 88987-0, Fax 88987-32
H Sacher Salzburg, Schwarzstr. 5-7, ✆ 88977, VI
H Austrotel Salzburg, Paris-Lodron-Str. 1, ✆ 881688, VI
H Bayrischer Hof, Kaiserschützenstr. 1, ✆ 4697-0, VI
H Austria Trend Hotel Europa, Rainerstr. 31, ✆ 889930, VI
H Kasererbräu, Kaig. 33, ✆ 8424450, VI

H Lasserhof, Lasserstr. 47, ✆ 873388, VI
H Schaffenrath, Alpenstr. 115, ✆ 639000, VI
H Eva-Maria, Sinnhubstr. 25, ✆ 829254, VI
H Hohenstauffen, Elisabethstr. 19, ✆ 872193, VI
H Weisses Kreuz, Bierjodlg. 6, ✆ 845641, VI
H Billroth, Billrothstr. 10-18, ✆ 93030-70, V
H Weiße Taube, Kaig. 9, ✆ 842404, V
H Arthotel Blaue Gans, Getreideg. 43, ✆ 841317, V
H Austria, Linzer G. 76, ✆ 872313, V
H Herbert, Nonntaler Hauptstr. 85, ✆ 820308, IV
H Lilienhof, Siezenheimerstr. 62, ✆ 433630, III
H Noppinger, Maxglaner Hauptstr. 29, ✆ 834034, III
H Riedenburg, Neutorstr. 31, ✆ 831223, III
Gh Plainbrücke, Itzlinger Hptstr. 91, ✆ 451728, V
Gh Überfuhr, Ignaz-Rieder-Kai 43, ✆ 623010, V
Gh Kirchenwirt, Kirchenstr. 22, ✆ 459448, V
Gh Schwarzes Rössl, Priesterhausg. 6, ✆ 874426, V
P Künstlerhaus, Hinterholzer Kai 2a, ✆ 0664/3415728, IV
P Sandwirt, Lastenstr. 6a, ✆ 874351, II
Pz Bloberghof, Hammerauer Straße 4, ✆ 830227, II
Pz Götzinger, Moosstr. 156, ✆ 826298, II
Pz Haslauer, Moosstr. 142, ✆ 830764, II
Pz Strasser, Moosstr. 186a, ✆ 824921, II
Pz Schneider, Schwedenstr. 18, ✆ 834362, II

109

Pz Zöller, Moosstr. 64, ☎ 832009, II

🏠 Jugend- & Familiengästehaus Salzburg, Josef-Preis-Allee 18, ☎ 842670-0, I (ganzjährig)

🏠 Jugendherberge Eduard-Heinrich-Haus, Eduard-Heinrich-Str. 2, ☎ 625976, I (ganzjährig)

🏠 Jugendherberge Haunspergstr., Haunspergstr. 27, ☎ 875030, ÖZ: Juli/Aug., I

🏠 Jugendherberge YO-HO, Paracelsusstr. 9, ☎ 879649, ganzjährig geöffnet, I

⛺ Camping Stadtblick, Rauchenbichlerstr. 21, ☎ 450652, Fax 458018, ÖZ: 20. März bis 15. Nov., April-12. Dez. 2004, 28. Dez.-8. Jan. 2005.

⛺ Camping Schloss Aigen, Weberbartlweg 20, ☎ 622079, ÖZ: Mai bis Sept.

⛺ Camping Kasern (Jägerwirt), Carl-Zuckmayer-Str. 26, ☎ 450576, ÖZ: 1. April bis 31. Okt.

⛺ Camping „Nord-Sam", Samstr. 22a, ☎ 660494, ÖZ: April 1- Sept. 30

Eugendorf
Postal code: 5301; Tel. area code: 06225

ℹ Tourismusverband, Salzburger Str. 7, ☎ 8424, Fax 7773

H Santner, Alte Wiener Str. 1, ☎ 8214-0, V

Gh Drei Eichen, Kirchbergstr. 1, ☎ 8521, V-VI

Gh Gchirnwirt, Alte Wiener Str. 49, ☎ 8229, V-VI

Gh Schwaighofwirt, Schwaighofenstr. 20, ☎ 06221/7733, IV

Gh Neuhofen, Neuhofenweg 2, ☎ 8392, III

Gh Zur Straß, Salzburger Str. 25, ☎ 8218, III-IV

Gh Holznerwirt, Dorf 4, ☎ 8205, V-VI

Gh Alpenblick, Schwaighofenberg 11, ☎ 8213, III

Gh Dachsteinblick, Bergweg 2, ☎ 8289, IV

Gh Gastagwirt, Alte Wiener Str. 37, ☎ 8231, V

Gh Neuwirt, Dorf 16, ☎ 8207, IV-V

P Schwaighofen, Sonnleitenstr. 3, ☎ 06221/7713, III-V

P Stettenhof, Stettnerstr. 26, ☎ 8314, III-IV

P Wallersee, Kirchenstr. 37, ☎ 8282, IV

P Sonnenhof, Sonnleitenstr. 9, ☎ 06221/7722, III

Pz Aspacher, Salzburger Str. 53, ☎ 7186, I

Pz Kaserer, Kirchenstr. 7, ☎ 8234, II

Pz Haus Kirchberg, Wiener Str. 42, ☎ 8612, II

Pz Leberbauer, Schopperweg 8, ☎ 2119, I-II

Pz Radauer, Dorf 15, ☎ 7646, II

Pz Schäffert, Reitberg 124, ☎ 7125, II

Pz Schmiedbauer, Schwaighofenstr. 15, ☎ 06221/7245, II

Pz Wintersteller, Reitbergstr. 4, ☎ 7744, II

Pz Freundlinger, Reitbergstr. 10, ☎ 8630, II

Seekirchen am Wallersee
Postal code: 5201; Tel. area code: 06212

ℹ Tourismusverband, Hauptstr. 2, ☎ 4035

Hg Flachauer Hof, Hauptstr. 50, ☎ 2267, III

Gh Zur Post, Hauptstr. 19, ☎ 2229, IV

Gh Bräu, Anton-Windhager-str. 2, ☎ 7997, III

Gh Brückenstüberl, Henndorfer Str. 1, ☎ 2398, III

Gh Hirschenwirt, Hauptstr. 54, ☎ 2203, III

Gh Zipfwirt, Seeburgerstr. 2, ☎ 2301, II-III

Gh Zur Seeburg, Seewalchen 4, ☎ 2385, III

P Mödlham, Untermödlham, ☎ 6163, II-III

⛱ Frauenlob-Prieswasser, Strandbad, ☎ 4088, open: May-Sept.

⛺ Strandcamping Zell am Wallersee, ☎ 4080, open: May-Sept.

Thalgau
Postal code: 5303; Tel. area code: 06235

ℹ Tourismusverband Thalgau, Marktplatz 4, ☎ 7350, Fax 6128

H Schwabenwirt, Marktpl. 7, ☎ 7422, III

Gh Santner, Salzburger Str. 10, ☎ 7216, IV

Gh Betenmacher, Unterdorf 1, ☎ 7328, III

P Huber, Ischlerbahnstr. 28, ☎ 6662, III

P Walburga, Vetterbach 37, ☎ 7378, III

P Scherrer, Vetterbach 18, ☎ 7476, II

P Aichriedler, Leithen 16, ☎ 5238, II

Pz Grubinger, Unterdorf 158, ☎ 6175, II

St. Gilgen
Postal code: 5340; Tel. area code: 06227

ℹ Tourismusverband, Mondsee Bundesstraße 1A, ☎ 2348, Fax 2348-9

H Hollweger, Mondsee-Bundesstr. 2, ☎ 2226-0

H Kendler, Kirchenpl. 3, ☎ 2223, V

H Jodlerwirt, Aberseestr. 39, ☎ 2511, V

P Radetzky, Streicherpl. 1, ☎ 2232, V

H Traube, Aberseestr. 4-6, ☎ 2254, IV

Hg Schernthaner, Schwarzenbrunnerstr. 4, ☎ 2402, III

Gh Zur Post, Mozartpl. 8, ☎ 2157, V

Gh Tirol, Aberseestr. 9, ☎ 2317, V

Gh Stern, Mozartpl. 3, ☎ 2249, IV

Gh Bachwirt, Steinklüftstr. 5, ☎ 20321, IV

P Salzkammergut, Helenenstr 19, ☎ 2511, V

P Wenglhof, Wenglstr. 1, ☎ 2476, IV

P Ferstl, Ischler Str. 1, ☎ 2216, III

P Falkensteiner, Salzburger Str. 11-13, ☎ 2395, III

P Mozartblick, Pöllach 23, ☎ 2403, III

P Bergdoktor, Leopold-Ziller-Str. 6, ☎ 8161-0, II

P Seeblick, Pöllach 29, ☎ 2682, II

Pz Mayerhofer, Salzburger Str. 9b, ☎ 2676, II

Pz Haus Helene, Brunnleitweg 20, ☎ 2310, II

⛺ Camping Birkenstrand, Schwand, ☎ 3029

⛺ Camping Lindenstrand, Schwand 19, ☎ 3205

⛺ Seecamping Primus, Schwand 39, ☎ 3228

🏠 Jugendherberge, Mondsee Str. 7-9, ☎ 2365, I

Mondsee
Postal code: 5310; Tel. area code: 06232

ℹ Tourismusverband, Dr.-Müller-Str. 3, ☎ 2270, Fax 4470

H Leitnerbräu, Steinerbachstr. 6, ☎ 6500, VI

H Königshof, Am See 28, ☎ 5627, VI

H Krone, Rainerstr. 1, ☎ 2236, IV

Hg Stabauer, Salzburger Str. 2, ☎ 2285, III

Gh Rössl-Stubn, Rainerstr. 32, ☎ 2235, IV

Gh Schlössl, Herzog-Odilo-Str. 92, ☎ 2390, IV

Gh Blaue Traube, Marktpl. 1, ✆ 2237, II
Gh Grüner Baum, Herzog-Odilo-Str. 39, ✆ 2314, II
Gh Zur grünen Eiche, Keuschen 53, ✆ 2130, II
Gh Drachenwand, St. Lorenz 32, ✆ 3356, III
Gh Weisse Taube, St. Lorenz 116, ✆ 2277, III
P Oberberger, Au 23, ✆ 3458, III
P Hemetsberger, Seebadstr. 1, ✆ 4934, III
P Göschlberger, Rainerstr. 58, ✆ 2218, III
P Meingast, Bader-Göbl-Str. 2, ✆ 2427, III
P Hochkreuz, Herzog-Odilo-Str. 63, ✆ 2614, II
P Am Schober, Keuschen 120, ✆ 2976, II
P Ellerhof, St. Lorenz 4, ✆ 4931, II
P Hildegard, St. Lorenz 268, ✆ 3006, I
🏠 Jugendherberge, Krankenhausstr. 9, ✆ 2418, I
🏕 Austria Camp, St. Lorenz, ✆ 2927,
open: May 1. - Sept. 30.

Henndorf
Postal code: 5302; Tel. area code: 06214
ℹ Tourismusverband, Hauptstr. 65, ✆ 6011
Gh Gersbachwirt, Wiener Str. 51, ✆ 8372, IV-V
P Brieger, Wiener Str. 60-62, ✆ 8373, IV-V
P Schroffnergut, Wankham 6, ✆ 6005
P Günther, Egon-Kornauth-Weg 6, ✆ 8447
P Stöllinger, Hauptstr. 99, ✆ 6120
P Zum Imker, Gartenstr. 8, ✆ 6479
Pz Juranka, Hankham 17, ✆ 8565
Pz Pohl, Roland-Fuß-Weg 7, ✆ 6831
Pz Schwaiger, Fenning 127, ✆ 7561

Pz Kressnigg, Westhöhenstr. 4, ✆ 20229
Pz Krug-Wieder, Enzing 22, ✆ 8520
Pz Höller, Schoarerbergstr. 43, ✆ 8482
Bh Hofbauer, Fenning 16, ✆ 7331
Bh Großsulzberg, Hof 13, ✆ 7442
Bh Joglbauer, Hof 22, ✆ 6884
Bh Streimling, Fenning 24, ✆ 8512
Bh Mühlholzbauer, Mühlholzbauerweg 22, ✆ 7419
🏕 Fenninger Spitz, Fenningerspitz, ✆ 8443

Neumarkt am Wallersee
Postal code: 5202; Tel. area code: 06216
ℹ Tourismusverband, Hauptstr. 30, ✆ 6907, Fax 7324
H Winkler, Thalham 12, ✆ 5270, III
Gh Krone, Hauptstr. 14, ✆ 5224, II
Gh Lerchenfeld, Lerchenfelderstr. 17, ✆ 4530, II
Gh Eggerberg, Neufahrn 22, ✆ 6711, II
Gh Lauterbacher, Schalkham 67, ✆ 4456, II
P Herzog, Maierhofstr. 19, ✆ 4519, I
🏕 Seecamp, Uferstr. 3, ✆ 4400, ÖZ: 1. 5. - 31. 10.

Oberhofen am Irrsee
Postal code: 4894; Tel. area code: 06213
ℹ Tourismusverband, Nr. 12, ✆ 8273
Gh Fischhof, Fischhof 30, ✆ 8202, II
P Lettner, Fischhof 9, ✆ 8316, II
P Bahn, Laiter 51, ✆ 8264, II
P Fischinger, Rabenschwand 31, ✆ 8360, II
P Krempler, Gegend 2, ✆ 7161, II
🏕 Moosmühle, Laiter 18, ✆ 8389

Strasswalchen
Postal code: 5204; Tel. area code: 06215
ℹ Tourismusverband, Salzburger Str. 26, ✆ 6420, Fax 5455
H Gasthof Weichenberger, Braunauerstr. 5, ✆ 8238, IV
H Gasthof „Zum Lebzelter", Marktplatz 1, ✆ 8206, IV-V
H Gasthof Zur Post, Marktpl. 9, ✆ 8207, III
Gh Landgasthof Haushofer, Brunn 2, ✆ 8243, III
Gh Gugg, Marktpl. 1, ✆ 8206, III
Gh Eder's, Braunauer Str. 5, ✆ 8238, III
Gh Landgasthof Schinwald, Irrsdorf 1, ✆ 6034, II
Gh Kreuzerwirt, Steindorf 35, ✆ 8310, II
Gh Pension „Zum Grünen Baum", Irrsdorf 6, ✆ 6037, III
Gh Ederbauer, Voglhub 3, ✆ 8380, III
Gh Gerbl, Linzer Str. 10, ✆ 8263, II
Gh Badinger, Hüttenedt 1, ✆ 06213/8557, I, 🐾
P Reisinger, Hüttenedt 48, ✆ 06213/7106, I
P Wirglauer, Watzlberg 40, ✆ 8462, VI

Köstendorf
Postal code: 5203; Tel. area code: 06216
ℹ Tourismusverband, Nr. 54, ✆ 7688, Fax 7688-4
P Freizeitcenter Köstendorf, Köstendorfer Landstr., ✆ 7688, III
Pz Prossinger, Ortszentrum, ✆ 6286, I, 🐾

Schleedorf „Schaudorf"
Postal code: 5205; Tel. area code: 06216
ℹ Tourismusverband, Dorf 95, ✆ 6911

🏛 Gemeindeamt Schleedorf, Dorf 104, ✆ 4100
Gh Hofwirt, Dorf 5, ✆ 6572
Gh Kollerwirt, Dorf 71, ✆ 657
Pz Költringer, Mölkham 123, ✆ 06217/6359
Pz Altmann, Engerreich 2, ✆ 06217/5447
Pz Franz und Paula Kronberger, Schleedorf 98, ✆ 6637, I
Pz Georg und Kathi Fuchs, Wallsberg 7, ✆ 6195
Pz Rosi Gruber, Schleedorf 115, ✆ 5142, I
Pz Otto und Erna Thalmayer, Schleedorf 15, ✆ 6565
Bh Reisingerhof, Reisach 2, ✆ 6195, I

Mattsee
Postal code: 5163; Tel. area code: 06217
ℹ Tourismusverband Mattsee, ✆ 6080
H Seewirt, Seestr. 4, ✆ 5455 od. 5271, VI
H Schloss Bräu, Mattsee 4, ✆ 5205, V
Gh Kapitelwirt, Marktplatz 7, ✆ 5203, IV
Gh Fürst, Aug. 01, ✆ 5400, III
Gh Mitterhof, Mitterhof 4, ✆ 5570
Gh Moorbad, Moorbad 1, ✆ 5238, III
P Altendorfer, Münsterholzstr. 66, ✆ 6028
P Baumgartlinger, Burghard Breitnerweg 11, ✆ 7601
P Kranzinger, Anzing 1, ✆ 5527, III
P Strasser, Münsterholzstr. 24, ✆ 5406, III
P Wagner, Weyer 4, ✆ 20207, III
P Wartstein, Burghard Breitnerweg 7, ✆ 7079, II
Pz Strasser, Wolf Dietrichweg 14, ✆ 5321, III
Pz Anzinger, Seewinkel 11, ✆ 5125, II

Pz Lindner, Diabelliweg 6, ✆ 7076, II
Pz Witzmann, Wolf Dietrichweg 11, ✆ 5380, II
Pz Strasser, Wolf Dietrichweg 3, ✆ 5585, I
Pz Feichtner, Fisching 5, ✆ 5445

Perwang am Grabensee
Postal code: 5163; Tel. area code: 06217
🛈 Tourismusverband, Nr. 4, ✆ 8247, Fax 8247-15
Gh Schachner-Neuwirt, Nr. 6, ✆ 8266, III
Pz Schäffer, Nr. 96, ✆ 8503, II
Pz Villa Gaudii, Nr. 94, ✆ 8847, II
Pz Weitgasser, Nr. 102, ✆ 8359, II
Pz Renzl, Nr. 61, ✆ 8277, II, 🗙
Pz Hofer, Nr. 57, ✆ 8296, II, 🗙
🏕 Camping Perwang, Grabensee 4, ✆ 8288, 8247

Seeham
Postal code: 5164; Tel. area code: 06217
🛈 Tourismusverband Seeham, Dorf 5, ✆ 5493
H Walkner, Eisenharting 4, ✆ 5550, V
H Altwirt, Seeham 1, ✆ 6120, V
H Sporthof Wimmer, Seeham 229, ✆ 7297, IV
Gh Entenwirt, Hauptstr. 61, ✆ 7110, IV
Gh Schießentobelhof, Matzing 19, ✆ 5386, III
Gh Grabensee, Seeham 201, ✆ 5384, II
P Stiedlbauerhof, Dürnbergerstr. 26, ✆ 5303, II
P Oitner, Seeham 79, ✆ 5589, I
Pz Dreiseenblick, Dürnbergerstr. 163, ✆ 5297, II
Pz Lindner, Wiesenbergstr. 4, ✆ 5539
🏕 Camping Wimmer, ✆ 7297

Obertrum
Postal code: 5162; Tel. area code: 06219
🛈 Tourismusverband, Mattigplatz 1, ✆ 6307 20474
Gh Neumayr, Dorfpl. 8, ✆ 6302, III
Gh Schmiedkeller, Kothgumprechting 27, ✆ 6564, II
P Fischerhof, Seestr. 15, ✆ 6358, II
P Rotschernhof, Rotschernweg 2, ✆ 7670, II
Pz Anglberger, Rotschernweg 1, ✆ 8214, I
Pz Grabner, Seestr. 16, ✆ 6263
🏕 Strandcamping, Seestr. 16, ✆ 6442, 6263

Anthering
Postal code: 5102; Tel. area code: 06223
🛈 Tourismusverband, Dorfstr. 1, ✆ 2279
H Ammerhauser, Dorfstr. 1, ✆ 2204, V
H Hammerschmiede, Acharting 22, ✆ 2503, V
Gh Vogl, Dorfplatz 2, ✆ 2214, II
P Villa Loretta, Pfarrhofweg 5, ✆ 2503, V
Pz Spitzauer, Bergstr. 11, ✆ 2332 bzw. 2900, II
Pz Hiesel, Wasserfeldstr. 26, ✆ 0664/5412879, II
Pz Haus Waldau, Bahnhofstr. 20, ✆ 2213, II 🗙
Pz Luginger, Reinthalweg 1, ✆ 23063, II 🗙
Bh Neuwirtbauer, Bahnhofstr. 21, ✆ 2219, II
Bh Christerbauer, Bahnhofstr. 24, ✆ 2312, II
Bh Hutzingerbauer, Trainting 12, ✆ 3333, II

Eugendorf
Postal code: 5301; Tel. area code: 06225
🛈 Tourismusverband, Salzburger Str. 9, ✆ 8424, Fax 7773

H Landhotel-Gasthof Drei Eichen, Kirchbergstr. 1, ✆ 8521, V-VI
H Landhotel Santner, Alte Wiener Str. 1, ✆ 8214-0, V
H Pension Schwaighofen, Sonnleitenstr. 3, ✆ 7713, III-IV
H Pension Wallersee, Kirchenstr. 37, ✆ 8282, IV
Gh Gastagwirt, Alte Wiener Str. 37, ✆ 8231, V-VI
Gh Gschirnwirt, Alte Wienerstr. 49, ✆ 8229, V-VI
Gh Holznerwirt, Dorf 4, ✆ 8205, V-VI
Gh Alpenblick, Schwaighofenberg 11, ✆ 8213, III
Gh Berghof Dachsteinblick, Bergweg 2, ✆ 8289, IV-V
Gh Neuwirt, Dorf 16, ✆ 8207, IV
Gh Berggasthof Schwaighofwirt, Schwaighofenstraße 20, ✆ 7733, IV
Gh Neuhofen, Neuhofenweg 2, ✆ 8392, III
Gh Zur Straß, Salzburger Str. 25, ✆ 8218, III-IV
P Stettenhof, Stettnerstr. 26, ✆ 8314, III-IV
P Heubergrand, Salzburger Str. 11, ✆ 8225, II
P Sonnenhof, Sonnleitenstr. 9, ✆ 7722, III
Pz Margarethe Ablinger, Ischlerbahnstr. 3, ✆ 8248, II
Pz Johanna Aspacher, Salzburger Str. 53, ✆ 7186I-II
Pz Elisabeth Feldbacher, Reitberg 205, ✆ 2189, I-II
Pz Elisabeth Frauenlob, Alte Wiener Str. 58, ✆ 8605, I-II
Pz Haus Kaserer, Kirchenstraße 7, ✆ 8234, II
Pz Haus Kirchberg, Wiener Str. 42, ✆ 8612, II
Pz Elisabeth Krenner, Rosenweg 3, ✆ 8607, I-II
Pz Notburga Leberbauer, Schopperweg 8, ✆ 2119, II

Pz Wolfgang u. Rosie Schäffert, Reitberg 124, ✆ 7125, II
Pz Hilde Traschwandtner, Kraihammerstr. 26, ✆ 2275, II
Pz Amilia Wallner, Kraiwiesen 26, ✆ 2224, I
Pz Maria Wintersteller, Reitbergstr. 4, ✆ 7744, II
Pz Maria Freundlinger, Reitbergstr. 10, ✆ 8630, II
Pz Anna Gstöttner, Dorf 18, ✆ 8220, I
Pz Maria Kittl, Schamingstr. 21, ✆ 2106, I-II
Pz Monika Kittl, Freilingweg 4, ✆ 7570, II
Pz Veronika Kittl, Kirchbergstr. 10, ✆ 2235, I-II
Pz Andreas Radauer, Dorf 15, ✆ 7646, II
Pz Maria Taglöhner, Burgstall 22, ✆ 8452, I-II
Pz Hiesel, Wasserfeldstr. 26, ✆ 2869, II
Pz Spitzauer, Bergstr. 11, ✆ 2332, I

Oberndorf
Postal code: 5110; Tel. area code: 06272
🛈 Tourismusverband, Stille-Nacht-Platz 2, ✆ 4422, Fax 4422-4
Gh Salzachhof, Brückenstr. 14, ✆ 4246, II
Gh Bauerenbräu, Salzburger Str. 149, ✆ 5422, II
Pz Permoser, Tettenbachstr. 3, ✆ 7509, II
Pz Schweigerer, Ziegeleistr. 12, ✆ 4369, II
Pz Wagner, Ziegeleistr. 9, ✆ 7597, I

St. Pantaleon
Postal code: 5120; Tel. area code: 06277
🛈 Tourismusverband, Gemeindeamt, ✆ 213-0, Fax 519

P Maria, Seestüberl, Seeleithen 21, ☎ 6688, II
P Großruck, Weyer 5, ☎ 6296, I
Pz Anthaner, Haigermoos 5, ☎ 8129, I

Laufen (D)
Postal code: 83410; Tel. area code: 08682
🛈 Verkehrsverband Abtsdorfer See, Im Schlossrondell 2,
☎ 1810 (Zimmervermittlung)
P Gästehaus Probst, Teisendorfer Str. 17, ☎ 1374, II
⛺ Camping, beim Strandbad Abtsdorfer See, 5 km
außerhalb von Laufen, südl. von Leobendorf,
☎ 89870

Freilassing (D)
Postal code: 83395; Tel. area code: 08654
H Gasthof Moosleitner, Wasserburger Str. 52, § 63060
🚭

Bergheim
Postal code: 5101; Tel. area code: 0662
Gh Bräuwirt, Lengfelden 21, ☎ 452163

Teisendorf
Postal code: 83317; Tel. area code: 08666
🛈 Tourismusbüro, Poststr. 14, ☎ 295
H Tiefenthaler Hof, Patting, Tiefenthal 16, ☎ 331
H Huberhof, Punschern 30, ☎ 1522
H Kolping, Dechantshof 3, ☎ 98590, IV-V
H Seidl, Holzhausen 2, ☎ 8010, V-VI
Gh Reiter, Achthal, ☎ 981328 🚭
Gh Mesnerwirt, Kirchplatz 1, Neukirchen, ☎ 7477
Gh Zur Post, Dorfstr. 20, Neukirchen, ☎ 564

Gh Schneck, Pfarrhofweg 20, Neukirchen, ☎ 356
Gh Ufering, Ufering 14, ☎ 220, II
Pz Groferbauer, Gumperting 21, ☎ 524, I
Pz Wimmer Elfriede, Roßdorf 8, ☎ 7466
Pz Helmingerhof, Hof 2, ☎ 7328, I 🚭

Neukirchen
Tel. area code: 08662
Pz Ramstötter Martha, Weitwies 37, ☎ 9615
Pz Ramstötter Helene, Weitwies 5, ☎ 7330
Pz Stehhuber Elisabeth, Lochmühle 1, ☎ 08666/355

Inzell
Postal code: 83334; Tel. area code: 08665
🛈 Inzeller Touristik GmbH, Rathausplatz 5, ☎ 9885-0,
Fax 988530
H Schmelz, Schmelzer Str. 132, ☎ 9870, V
H Sport Hotel Post, Reichenhaller Str. 2, ☎ 985222, VI
H Sport- und Ferienhotel Chiemgauer Hof, Lärchenstr. 5,
☎ 6700, VI
H Falkenstein, Kreuzfeldstr. 2, ☎ 98890, IV-V
H Restaurant Reiter, Lärchenstr. 2, ☎ 98100, II-IV
H Gasthaus Schwarzberg, Traunsteiner Str. 95, ☎ 7565,
III-IV
Hg Haus Andrea, Schmelzer Str. 21, ☎ 98640, IV
Hg Landhaus Bergblick, Rauschbergstr. 38, ☎ 98450,
III-IV
Hg Hubertus garni, Gamskogelstr. 24, ☎ 7382, IV-V
Hg Aparthotel garni Seidel, Lärchenweg 17, ☎ 98440,
IV-V

Gh Neimoar, Familie Gallinger, Schmelzer Straße 40,
☎ 7322 od. 7782, III
Gh Cafe Fischer, Sulzbacher 41, ☎ 7654, III
Gh Kienberg, Reichenhaller Str. 3, ☎ 223, IV
Gh Gästehaus Egger, Sulzbacher Str. 47, ☎ 7104, IV
Gh Boden, Traunsteiner Str. 152, ☎ 263, II
Gh Fantenberg, Salinenweg 83, ☎ 476, II
Gh Inzeller Hof, Bauhofstr. 7, ☎ 282, III
Gh Pension Kreuzfeld, Kreuzfeldstr. 6, ☎ 280, III
Gh Pension Rauschbergblick, Hutterer 4, ☎ 452, II
Gh Pension Vroni, Am Bichl 1, ☎ 268, III
Gh Café Zwing, Reichenhaller Str. 100, ☎ 275, II-III
P Saurler, Schmelzer Str. 60, ☎ 530, II
P Moorhof, Fam. Flatscher, Schmelzer Str. 46, ☎ 1647,
II
P Bavaria, Ahornstr. 8, ☎ 507, II-III
P Birkenhof, Birkenweg 20, ☎ 580, III-V
P Gästehaus Egger, Sulzbacher Str. 47, ☎ 7104, IV
P Gästehaus Erika, Traunsteiner Str. 73, ☎ 257, II
P Marianne, Eckerstr. 11, ☎ 7557, II
P Haus Stefanie, Reichenhaller Str. 66, ☎ 7510, II
P Gästehaus „beim Kreuzfeld", Kreuzfeldstr. 3, ☎ 6044,
II
P Landhaus Luise Dufter, Reichenhaller Str. 67,
☎ 7301, II
P Haus Hirschbichler, Adlgasser Str. 42, ☎ 307, II
P Gästehaus Maier-Gehmacher, Kreuzfeldstr. 1,
☎ 1661, II

P Gästehaus Mühlberger, Kreuzbaumstr. 23, ☎ 521, II
P Haus Pastötter, Am Kurpark 13, ☎ 7867, I
P Friedl Plenk, Adlgasser Str. 107, ☎ 7005, II
P Restner, Sulzbacher Str. 69, ☎ 7689, II
P Haus Rieder Josef, Adlgasser Str. 101, ☎ 7122, II
P Haus Schöneck, Eichenweg 14, ☎ 7177, II
P Schwaiger, Eckerstr. 35a, ☎ 1376, II
Pz Gästehaus Aicher, Sulzbacher Str. 89, ☎ 7883, II
Pz Haus Böhm, Eckerstr. 61, ☎ 929664, II
Pz Haus Dufter, Schwarzenberger Weg 11, ☎ 1582, II
Pz Haus Kress, Adlgasser Str. 103, ☎ 418, I
Pz Haus Scheurl, Froschseerstr. 20, ☎ 7359, II
Pz Gästehaus Schrittenlocher, Reichenhaller Str. 43,
☎ 7518, II

Reit im Winkl
Postal code: 83237; Tel. area code: 08640
🛈 Tourist-Information, Rathausplatz 1, ☎ 800-20 od.
☎ 800-21
H Unterwirt, Kirchplatz 2, ☎ 8010, VI
H Posthotel, Kirchplatz 7, ☎ 9870, V
H Zum Postillion, Dorfstr. 32-34, ☎ 98240, IV-VI
H Bichlhof, Tiroler/Alte Grenzstr. 1-3, ☎ 98250, III-V
H Am Hauchen, Am Hauchen 5-7, ☎ 8774, IV-V
H Edelweiß, Am Grünbühel 1, ☎ 98890, III-V
H Sonnwinkl, Kaiserweg 12, ☎ 98470, III-V
H Theresenhof, Hausbachweg 3, ☎ 8514, III-IV
Hg Lenzenhof, Am Kirchplatz 8, ☎ 493, III-V
Hg Weißes Rößl, Dorfstr. 19, ☎ 98230, III-V

113

Hg Kaindl, Schwimmbadstr. 2-4, ✆ 98260, III-IV

Hg Sonnhof's Ferienresidenz, Gartenstr. 3, ✆ 98800, IV-VI

Gh Zum Eichhof, Dorfstr. 37, ✆ 98440, III-V

P Angerer, Birnbacher Str. 1, ✆ 5011, III

P Alpenrose, Walmbergstr. 11, ✆ 98450, III-IV

P Am Kurparkweg, Dorfstr. 1, ✆ 8466, II-IV

P Lengg, Dorfstr. 5, ✆ 8507, II

P Pretzner, Dorfstr. 4, ✆ 97690, III

P Beim Rottmeister, Weitseestr. 20, ✆ 8650, II-III

P Sonnenhang, Birkenweg 2, ✆ 1387, II-III

Pz Vicktor, Hausbergstr. 18, ✆ 8513, II

Pz Haus Bergblick, Gartenstr. 5, ✆ 8322, I-II

Pz Haus Eva-Maria, Kaiserweg 8, ✆ 8118, II

Pz Haus Hauck, Alte Grenzstr. 7, ✆ 8624, II

Pz Haus Katharina, Weitseestr. 34, ✆ 8753, II-III

Groißenbach

⛺ Campingplatz, ✆ 98210

Schönram

Postal code: 83367; Tel. area code: 08686

Gh Bräustüberl Schönram, Salzburger Str. 10, ✆ 271, III

Pz Dürnberger, Salzburger Str. 38, ✆ 505, I ✖

Pz Gruber, Salzburger Str. 2, ✆ 529, I ✖

Petting

Postal code: 83367; Tel. area code: 08686

🛈 Tourist-Information, Hauptstr. 13, ✆ 200

Gh Götzinger, Seestr. 43, ✆ 8010, I-II

Gh Seehaus, Seehaus 3, ✆ 98810, III 🛌

Pz Riedl, Kirchfeldstr. 15, ✆ 224, I ✖

Pz Schmid, Kirchfeldstr. 7, ✆ 8570, I ✖

Kühnhausen

Postal code: 83367; Tel. area code: 08685

Pz Lucksch, Am Hang 1, ✆ 506, I ✖

Tettenhausen

Postal code: 83329; Tel. area code: 08681

⛺ Campingplatz, am Strandbad, ✆ 1622 od. ✆ 313

Waging am See

Postal code: 83329; Tel. area code: 08681

🛈 Tourist-Info, Salzburger Str. 32, ✆ 313

H Wölkhammer, Haslacher Weg 3, ✆ 4080, IV-VI

H Zum Unterwirt, Seestr. 23, ✆ 69330, III-V

H Zur Post, Seestr. 1, ✆ 210, IV

Gh Schmid, Wiesenweg 6, ✆ 4917, II

Gh Tanner, Hochfellnerstr. 17, ✆ 9219, II

P Tannenheim, Gaisbergstr. 14, ✆ 312, II

Pz Busch, Gaisbergstr. 4, ✆ 9892, I ✖

Pz Göstl, Adalbert-Stifter-Str. 28, ✆ 9671, II

Pz Mühlbacher, Traunsteiner Str. 7, ✆ 1235, II ✖

⛺ Strandcamping, Am See 1, ✆ 552 🛌

Nußdorf/Chiemgau

Postal code: D-83365; Tel. area code: 08669

🛈 Tourist-Information, Gemeindeverwaltung, Dorfplatz 15, ✆ 87370

Gh Zenz Sondermoning, Chieminger Str. 16, ✆ 6490, I-II

Chieming

Postal code: D-83339; Tel. area code: 08664

🛈 Tourist-Information Chieming, ✆ 9886-47

Gh Unterwirt, Hauptstr. 32, ✆ 98460, II-IV

Gh Goriwirt, Truchtlachingerstr. 1, Egerer, ✆ 98430, III

P Haus Gerti, Mühlenweg 1, ✆ 467, II-III

P Strudelmichel, Irmingardstr. 4, ✆ 985956, II-III

P Förster, Christelmal 8, ✆ 426, II

Pz Putz, Stötthamer Str. 12, ✆ 295, I-II

⛺ Möwenplatz-Chieming, Grabenstätterstr. 3, ✆ 361

⛺ Kupferschmiede, Arlaching, ✆ 08667/446

⛺ Seehäusl, Stöttham, ✆ 303

Seebruck

Postal code: 83358; Tel. area code: 08667

🛈 Tourist-Information Seebruck, ✆ 7139

H Post, Ludwig-Thoma-Str. 8, ✆ 8870, V

H Wassermann, Ludwig-Thoma-Str. 1, ✆ 8710, V-VI 🛌

P Seeblick, Traunsteiner Str. 55, ✆ 208, IV

Gh Cafe Kaltner, Traunsteiner Str. 4, ✆ 88820, IV-V

Gh Gartner, Ludwigstr. 3, ✆ 327, III-V

Pz Haus Josefine, Rosenheimer Str. 12, ✆ 7195, II

Pz Haus Schönbrunner, Lärchenweg 5, ✆ 7373, II

Pz Daxenberger, Lärchenweg 3, ✆ 344, II

⛺ Lambach, ✆ 7889

Truchtlaching

Postal code: 83376; Tel. area code: 08667

P Barbara, Brunnäckerstr. 1, ✆ 969, IV 🛌

Pz Haus Axthammer, ✆ 430

Bh Schlafen Im Heu, Wehrländerstraße 29, ✆ 7077 🛌

Seeon

Postal code: 83370; Tel. area code: 08624

🛈 Kultur- und Bildungszentrum, Klosterweg 1, ✆ 8970

Hg Haus Rufinus, Klosterweg 31, ✆ 875940, V

P Neuwirt, Altenmarkter Str. 19, ✆ 2504, III

Gh Haus Klosterblick „Cafe Helga", Weinbergstr. 56, ✆ 8969811, IV-V

Pz Fiedler, Weinbergstr. 18, ✆ 1298, II

Breitbrunn am Chiemsee

Postal code: 83254; Tel. area code: 08054

🛈 Tourist Information, Gollenhausener Str. 1, ✆ 234

Gh Beim Oberleitner, Seestr. 24, ✆ 396, III

Gh „Zum Koniwirt", Eggstätter Str. 11, ✆ 648

P Gradlhof, Badstr. 2, ✆ 218, III-IV

P Danglhof, Badstr. 3, ✆ 7107

P Jell Cilla, Seestr. 43, ✆ 383

P Wagnerhof, Anni Jell, Seestr. 31, ✆ 202

P Wagnerhof, Brigitte Jell, Seestr. 31, ✆ 90380

Bh Frank Juliane, Rimstinger Str. 6, ✆ 676

Eggstätt

Postal code: 83125; Tel. area code: 08056

🛈 Tourist-Info, Obinger Str. 7, ✆ 1500

H Linde, Priener Str. 42, ✆ 90559-0, IV-V

P Unterwirt, Kirchplatz 8, ✆ 337, III

Pz Lindner, Ahornstr. 8, ✆ 669, I-II ✖

Pz Vetter, Eichenstr. 3, ✆ 1759, I-II

Oberndorf
Pz Fischer, Oberndorf 12, ✆ 558, I-II

Oberulsham
Gh Zum Sägwirt, Oberulsham 5, ✆ 346, II-III

Amerang
Postal code: 83123; Tel. area code: 08075

🅸 Tourist-Info Amerang Bahnhofstr. 3, ✆ 9197-28
P Purzelbaum, Wasserburger Str. 17, ✆ 236, IV
P Gartlacher Hof, ✆ 08071/93552

Oberratting
Bh Ernstberger Christa, Oberratting 8, ✆ 9286, III

Prien am Chiemsee
Postal code: D-83209; Tel. area code: 08051

🅸 Kurverwaltung, Alte Rathausstr. 11, ✆ 69050
H Bayerischer Hof, Bernauer Str. 3, ✆ 6030, V
H Zum Fischer am See, Harrasser Str. 145, ✆ 90760, IV-V
H Möwe, Seestr. 111, ✆ 5004, III-IV
H Westernacher, Seestr. 115, ✆ 4722, III
P Haus Drexler, Seestr. 95, ✆ 4802, III
P Haus Scholze, Seestr. 52-54, ✆ 2687, II
P Händelmayer, Rafenauerweg 7, ✆ 2823, II
P Hasholzner, Dickertsmühlstr. 3, ✆ 2733, I-II
🅷 Jugendherberge, Carl-Braun-Str. 46, ✆ 68770
🅰 Campingplatz Hofbauer, Bernauer Str. 110, ✆4136

Harras
🅰 Campingplatz Harras, ✆ 90460 🈺

Rimsting
Postal code: D-83253; Tel. area code: 08051

🅸 Verkehrsamt, Schulstr. 4, ✆ 6876-21
H Zur Sonne, Endorfer Str. 27, ✆ 2053, II
P Westfalenhof, Priener Str. 8, ✆ 91900, II
P Hasenhof, Endorfer Str. 1, ✆ 2322 II

Schafwaschen
Gh Seehof, Schafwaschen 4, ✆ 1697, II-III

Stephanskirchen
Postal code: D-83071; Tel. area code: 08036

🅸 Verkehrsverein, ✆ 615
P Weinbergnest, Weinbergstr. 15, ✆ 2559, IV
Bh Hamberger, Fussenweg 61, ✆ 9482, II
Bh Forstner, Badzaunstr. 10, ✆ 7910, I-II
Bh Lechner, Baierbacher, ✆ 4827 II
Fw Schmiedmoarhof, Simsseestr. 369, ✆ 7853, II

Wasserburg am Inn
Postal code: D-83512; Tel. area code: 08071

🅸 Verkehrsamt der Stadt Wasserburg a. Inn, Salzsenderzeile, Rathaus, ✆ 10522
H Fletzinger, Fletzingerg. 1, ✆ 90890, V 🈺
H Paulaner-Stuben, Marienpl. 9, ✆ 3903, II-III
P Pichlmayr, Burgau Nord, Anton-Woger-Str. 2-4, ✆ 40021, IV-V
Gh Huberwirt, Salzburger Str. 25, ✆ 7433, IV-V
P Staudham, Münchner Str. 30, ✆ 7435, VI
Pz Pfeiffer, Schloss Weikertsham, ✆ 51338, IV-V

Griesstätt
Postal code: 83556; Tel. area code: 08039

🅸 Gemeindeamt, Innstr. 4, ✆ 9056-0
H Abaton, Laiming 12, ✆ 909880, V
P Jagerwirt, Wasserburger Str. 7, ✆ 3782, III
Pz Hobelsberger Erika, Dr.-Mitterwieser Str. 7, ✆ 902688
Pz Schindler Franz u. Ute, Schulstr. 7, ✆ 908395

Vogtareuth
Postal code: D-83569; Tel. area code: 08038

Gh Vogtareuther Hof, Krankenhausstr. 3, ✆ 258, II
Pz Berghammer, Hofstätt 3, ✆ 08031/71945
Pz Elisabeth Huber, Wasserburger Str. 5, ✆ 396, I
Pz Dutz, Sonnenstr. 8, ✆ 452
Pz Kaffl, Farmach 1, ✆ 403

Rott am Inn
Postal code: D-83543; Tel. area code: 08039

🅸 Gemeindeverwaltung Rott am Inn, Kaiserhof 3, ✆ 9068-0
Gh Zur Post, Marktpl. 5, ✆ 1225, II
Gh Am Kirchplatz, Marktpl. 2, ✆ 1222, II
Gh Lengdorfer Hof, Lengdorf 30, ✆ 409602, II

Schechen
Postal code: D-83135; Tel. area code: 08039

🅸 Gemeindeverwaltung Schechen, Rosenheimer Str. 13, ✆ 90670
Gh Egger-Stüberl, Rosenheimerstr. 17, ✆ 90390, III
🅰 Campingplatz am Erlensee, ✆ 2935

Marienberg
Gh Mesnerwirt, Marienberg 4, ✆ 08031/28480, IV-VI

Rosenheim
Postal code: 83022, .24, .26; Tel. area code: 08031

🅸 Touristinfo, am Ticketcenter, Stollstraße 1, Postadresse: D-83022 Kufsteiner Str. 4, ✆ 3659061
H Alpenhotel Wendelstein, Bahnhofstr. 4-6, ✆ 33023
Gh Hammerwirt, Kufsteiner Str. 29, ✆ 235451
Gh Kastenauer Hof, Birkenweg 20, ✆ 62158, II-III
Gh Flötzinger Bräu, Kaiserstr. 5, ✆ 31714, IV
Postal code: 83024
Gh Höhensteiger, Westerndorfer Str. 101, ✆ 86667, II-III
Gh Alt Fürstätt, Fürstätt 17, ✆ 24490, IV
Postal code: 83026
H Fortuna, Hochplattenstr. 42, ✆ 616363, V
Gh Happinger Hof, Happinger Str. 23, ✆ 616970, II
P Hubertus, Seestr. 49, ✆ 66236, II-IV 🈺

Neubeuern
Postal code: D-83115; Tel. area code: 08035

🅸 Verkehrsamt, Marktpl. 4, ✆ 2165.
H Burghotel, Marktpl. 23, ✆ 2456, III-IV
H Hofwirt, Marktpl. 5, ✆ 2340, III
Pz Stelzer, Färberstr. 2 a, ✆ 4775

Nußdorf am Inn
Postal code: D-83131; Tel. area code: 08034

🅸 Verkehrsamt, Brannenburgerstr. 10, ✆ 907920
Gh Ring-Stüberl, Am Ring 1, ✆ 7573, II-III

Gh Schneiderwirt, Hauptstr. 8, ☏ 4527, III
P Sonne, Hochriesweg 7, ☏ 3030, III
P Staber, Mühltalweg 22, ☏ 2335, IV
P Ueffing, Bugscheinw. 3, ☏ 8531, III-V
Pz Auer, Hochriesweg 1, ☏ 8841, I
Pz Schweinsteiger, Kranzhornweg 5, ☏ 7283, II
Bh Zacherlhof, Hauptstr. 16, ☏ 708835, II
Bh Brandstetter Hof, Pfarrhofweg 4, ☏ 2603, II

Oberaudorf

Postal code: D-83080; Tel. area code: 08033
ℹ️ Touristinfo, Kufsteiner Str. 6, ☏ 301-20
H Sporthotel Wilder Kaiser, Naunspitzstr. 1, ☏ 9250, V
H Feuriger Tatzlwurm, Tatzlwurm 1, ☏ 08034/30080, V
H Hotel am Rathaus, Kufsteiner Str. 4, ☏ 1470, IV
H Keindl, Dorfstr. 2-4, ☏ 30400, V
H Bayerischer Hof, Sudelfeldstr. 12, ☏ 92350, IV 🛏
H Alpenhof, Rosenheimer Str. 97, ☏ 308180, V
H Aopenhotel Bernhards, Marienplatz 2, ☏ 30570, IV
Gh Ochsenwirt, Carl-Hagan-Str. 14, ☏ 30790, IV 🛏
Gh Kaiserblick, Kufsteiner Str. 12, ☏ 30580, III
P Schreyer, Auerburgstr. 4, ☏ 1803, II
P Wagnerhof, Carl-Hagan-Str. 1, ☏ 2381, III
P Gästehaus Kogeler, Bergstr. 3, ☏ 4296, III
P Kammerloher, Agger Str. 28, ☏ 2656, II
P Großfuchsenhof, Carl-Hagan-Str. 5, ☏ 1561, III
P Altes Schützenhaus, Schützenstr. 3, ☏ 4582, III
P Gästehaus Böhm, Dorfstr. 3, ☏ 1513, II

Niederndorf

Postal code: A-6342; Tel. area code: 05373
ℹ️ Tourismusverband, Nr. 32, ☏ 61377
Gh Tiroler Hof, Nr. 209 beim Zollamt, ☏ 61213, II
Gh Kuhstall, Nr. 92, ☏ 61287, I-II
Gh Stadler, Nr. 63, ☏ 61323, II
P Schwaiger, Nr. 64, ☏ 61403, I
P Thrainer, Nr. 98, ☏ 61506, I
Pz Achorner, Nr. 58 b, ☏ 61050
Pz Holl, Nr. 281, ☏ 61720

Kufstein

Postal code: A-6330; Tel. area code: 05372
ℹ️ Tourismusverband, Münchner Str. 2, ☏ 62207.
H Andreas Hofer, Georg-Pirmoserstr. 8, ☏ 6980, V
H Auracher Löchl, Römerhofg. 3-5, ☏ 62138, IV
H Kufsteiner Hof, Franz-Josefs-Pl. 1, ☏ 71030, IV
H Lanthalerhof, Schopperweg 28, ☏ 64105, III
H Sporthotel, Feldg. 35, ☏ 64732, IV
H Zipferkeller, Marktg. 14a, ☏ 62396, III
H Gisela, Bahnhofpl. 4, ☏ 64520, II
Gh Stimmersee, Stimmersee 22, ☏ 62756, II
Gh Kirchenwirt, Zeller Str. 17, ☏ 62512, I-II
P Haus Maier, Mitterndorfer Str. 13, ☏ 62260, II
P Ganderhof, Weißachstr. 41, ☏ 62432, II
P München, Inng. 14, ☏ 64775, III
🏔 Beim Hotel „Zum Bären", Salurner Str. 36,
    ☏ 62229, May-late Sept.

Walchsee

Postal code: 6344; Tel. area code: 05374
ℹ️ Tourist-Information, Dorfplatz 10, ☏ 52230
🏔 Seespitz, Seespitz 1, ☏ 5359
🏔 Ferienpark Süd-See, ☏ 5339
🏔 Seemühle, Am See 3, ☏ 5458

Waidach

Postal code: 6345; Tel. area code: 05375
H Waidachhof, Waidach 22, ☏ 6415, IV-V

Kössen

Postal code: A-6345; Tel. area code: 05375
ℹ️ Tourismusverband Kössen-Schwendt, Infobüro, Dorf 15, ☏ 6287
H Post, Dorf 43, ☏ 29490, V
H Alpina, Außerkapelle 2, ☏ 2146, V-VI
H Golf&Sporthotel Tyrol, Dorf 12, ☏ 6241, V-VI
H Sonneck, Außerkapelle 2, ☏ 6453, V-VI
Gh Dorfstadl, Dorf 22, ☏ 6504, III
Gh Hüttwirt, Hütte 33, ☏ 6210, III
Gh Erzherzog Rainer, Dorf 10, ☏ 6242, III
P Landegger, Feldweg 7, ☏ 6528, II-III
P Gästehaus Oberbach, Thurnbichl 52, ☏ 6260, II-III
P Rottenspacher, Leitweg 9, ☏ 6425, II
P Gästehaus Radetzky, Hüttfeldstr. 14, ☏ 6263, II
P Brunner, Postweg 13, ☏ 6466, II
P Haus Central, Dorf 38, ☏ 6322, II
P Gieringer, Schwimmbadweg 6, ☏ 6397, II
P Marianne, Dorf 18, ☏ 6284, II

P Alpengruß, Feldweg 9, ☏ 6304, II
P Haus Sonnleit, Leitweg 29, ☏ 6434, II
P Hosp, Hüttfeldstr. 6, ☏ 6336, III
P Talin, Bergfeld 9, ☏ 6271, II
Pz Haus Anna, Alleestr. 12a, ☏ 6601, II
Pz Haus Schreder, Dorf 29, ☏ 6288, II
Pz Haus Edith, Hüttenfeldstr. 56, ☏ 6637, II
Pz Haus Margit, Aleestr. 50, ☏ 6927, II
Pz Ambrusch, Steinbruchweg 4, ☏ 6364, II
Pz Foidl Stefan, Moserbergweg 33, ☏ 6573, II
Pz Gruber, Erlaustr. 41, ☏ 6188, II
Pz Bichler, Moserbergweg 16, ☏ 6531, I
Pz Kitzbichler, Alleestr. 67, ☏ 6327, II
Pz Lechthaler, Schwendterstr. 4, ☏ 6386, I
Pz Haus Montana, Kindergartenweg 6, ☏ 6454, II
Pz Scharnagl, Lendgasse 12, ☏ 6265, II
Pz Schermer, Alleestr. 26, ☏ 6274, II
Pz Schwaiger, Wiesenweg 19, ☏ 6631, II
Pz Singer, Feldweg 16, ☏ 6145, II
Pz Steinlechner Maria, Hüttfeldstr. 21, ☏ 2603, II

Bichlach

H Riedl, Bichlach 10, ☏ 6268, V-VI

Grundharting

Pz Hörfarter Johann u. Gerti, Gundharting 10, ☏ 6002, I-II

Leitwang

Pz Grandner Edeltraud, Leitwang 23, ☏ 2469, I

Waidach

H Waidachstuben, Waidach 22, ☏ 6415, IV
Gh Brennerwirt, Waidach 55, ☏ 6289, III

Schwendt

Postal code: 6345; Tel. area code: 05375

Gh Schwendterwirt, Dorf 4, ☏ 6716, IV
Gh Café Anneliese, Dorfstr. 15, ☏ 6006, IV
Gh Hohenkendl, Kohlenalstr. 23, ☏ 6810, IV
Gh Berggasthof Kohlalm, Dorf 4, ☏ 0676/9373955
P Restaurant Forellenhof, Kohlenalstr. 3, ☏ 29212, II
P Gästehaus Zita, Dorfstr. 51, ☏ 6797, II
P Café Schwendtner, Dorfstr. 61, ☏ 6043, II
P Haus Sonnenhügel, Kirchgasse 3, ☏ 6790
P Schwaiger Margarethe, Dorf 7, ☏ 2223, II
P Haus Wohlfartsstätter, Dorfstr. 20, ☏ 2320, II

Unterschwendt

P Ferienhof Unterhochstätt, Unterschwendt 21, ☏ 6475, IV-V

Niederachen

Postal code: 6345; Tel. area code: 05375

P Aigner, Niederachen 18, ☏ 6383, II

Kirchdorf i. Tirol

Postal code: 6382; Tel. area code: 05352

🛈 Tourismusverband, Litzlfeldner Str. 2, ☏ 6933
H Annahof, Innsbruckerstr. 59, ☏ 63155
H Seiwald, ☏ 3156

Waidring

Postal code: 6384; Tel. area code: 05353

🛈 Tourismusverband Waidring, Dorfstr. 12, ☏ 5242
H Waidringerhof, Dorfstr. 16, ☏ 5228, VI
Gh Waldstüberl, Schredergasse 8, ☏ 52011, III
P Chalet Tirol, Sonnwendstr. 19, ☏ 5942, II-III
🛆 Erich Kienpointer, Camping Steinplatte, ☏ 5345, Fax 5406

Lofer

Postal code: 5090; Tel. area code: 06588

🛈 Tourismusverband Sbg. Saalachtal, Lofer 310, ☏ 83210
H St. Hubertus, Lofer 180, ☏ 8266, IV-VI
H Das Bräu, Brüggler & Rainer, Lofer 28, ☏ 82070, V
H Lintner, Lofer 59, ☏ 8240, III-V
H Salzburger Hof, Lofer 128, ☏ 8333, III-V
H Dax, Lofer 250, ☏ 8339, IV-VI
Gh Neuwirt, Lofer 177, ☏ 8315, III
Gh Forellenstube, Lofer 7, ☏ 8377, III
Gh Landhaus Eva-Marie, Lofer 132, ☏ 8232, III-V
Gh Antonia, Au 26, ☏ 8604, II-III
Gh Sonnenhof, Lofer 241, ☏ 8354, II-IV
P Färberhaus, Lofer 10, ☏ 8258, II
P Herta, Lofer 158, ☏ 7214, II-III
P Bräuschmied, Lofer 147, ☏ 8647, III
P Egger, Lofer 16, ☏ 8205, II
P Mühlpointhof, Lofer 38, ☏ 82420, III-V
P Haus Bartlmä, Lofer 6, ☏ 8566, II
P Dankl, Lofer 207, ☏ 8625, II
P Alpengruß, Scheffsnoth 80+91, ☏ 8402, II
P Flatscherbauer, Scheffsnoth 5, ☏ 8686, II
P Tannenhof, Lofer 213, ☏ 8332, II-III
P Alpenheim, Lofer 259, ☏ 8300, II
P Edergut, Lofer 113, ☏ 8378, II
P Posthof, Lofer 133, ☏ 8325, II
P Tiefenthaler, Lofer 30, ☏ 8269, II
P Haus Leo (Vegetarian), Gumping 11, ☏ 7065, III (no smoking)
Pz Auer, Lofer 39, ☏ 8313, II
Pz Berger, Scheffsnoth 84, ☏ 8666, II
Pz Einwaller, Lofer 12, ☏ 8273, II
Pz Faistauer, Lofer 178, ☏ 8220, II-III
Pz Hinterseer, Scheffsnoth 3, ☏ 8401, II
Pz Tiefenthaler, Lofer 30, ☏ 8269, II
Pz Ebser, Lofer 284, ☏ 7207, II
Pz Kofler, Lofer 257, ☏ 8500, II
Pz Költringer, Lofer 252, ☏ 8429, II
Pz Patricia, Lofer 264, ☏ 8343, II
Pz Schweinöster, Au 39, ☏ 7487 od. 8604, II
🛆 Campingplatz Grubhof

Unken

Postal code: 5091; Tel. area code: 06589

🛈 Infostelle, ☏ 4202
Gh Schütterbad, ☏ 4296, IV-V
Gh „Zu den drei Brüdern", Reith 11, ☏ 4522, III-V
Gh Dietrichshorn, ☏ 4348, I-II
Gh Kinderhotel Post, ☏ 42260, III-IV
Gh Kirchenwirt, Niederland 3, ☏ 4204, III
Gh Friedlwirt, Gföll 28, ☏ 4265, II-III
Gh Heutaler Hof, Gföll 220, ☏ 8220, IV-V
Gh Wimmer, Unken 94, ☏ 4367, III-IV
Gh Heutal, Gföll 91, ☏ 8216, III-IV
Gh Hintergföll, Gföll 135, ☏ 8224, II-III
P Helga, Gföll 212, ☏ 4591, II
P Ensinger, Niederland 174, ☏ 4298, III-IV
P Dorfcafe, Niederland 255, ☏ 7156, III-IV
P Wildschütz, Unken 101, ☏ 4505, II-III
P Pfeiffer, Unken 28, ☏ 4307, II
Pz Seidl, Unken 44, ☏ 4353
Pz Wimmer, Reit 12, ☏ 4533
Pz Eder, Niederland 121, ☏ 4626, II
Pz Haus Elisabeth, Niederland 168, ☏ 4227, II
Pz Fernsebner, Niederland 60, ☏ 4219, II
Pz Fuchs Marie-Luise, Nr. 216, ☏ 7111
Bh Neuhauserbauer, Niederland 34, ☏ 4603, II
Bh Eggerbauer, Niederland 1, ☏ 4379
Bh Ennsmannbauer, Niederland 10, ☏ 4327
Bh Pichlerhof, Niederland 13, ☏ 4221
🛆 Camping „Werferbauer", Fam. Möschl, ☏ 4466

Bad Reichenhall

Postal code: 83435; Tel. area code: 08651

🛈 Kur- und Verkehrsverein e.V., Wittelsbacher Str. 15, ☏ 606-303
H Alpina, Adolf-Schmid-Str. 5, ☏ 9750, V
H Steigenberger, Salzburger Str. 2-6, ☏ 7770, VI
H Residenz Bavaria, Am Münster 3, ☏ 7760, VI 🛆

H Luisenbad, Ludwigstr. 33, ☎ 6040, VI
H Alpenrose, Luitpoldstr. 19, ☎ 97600, V
H Almrausch, Frühlingstr. 5, ☎ 96690, III-V
H Erika, Adolf-Schmid-Str. 3, ☎ 95360, IV-V
H Falter, Traunfeldstr. 8, ☎ 9710, V
H Hofwirt, Salzburger Str. 21, ☎ 98380, V
H Reseda, Mackstr. 2, ☎ 9670, III-IV
H Seeblick, Thumsee 10, ☎ 98630, V-VI
H Bürgerbräu, Rathausplatz, ☎ 6089, V-VI
H Hansi, Rinckstr. 3, ☎ 98310, IV-V ⌨
H Klosterhof, Steilhofweg 19, ☎ 98250, VI
H Oechsner, Am Thumsee 7, ☎ 96970, III
H Salzburger Hof, Mozartstr. 7, ☎ 97690, IV-V
H Friedrichshöhe, Adolf-Schmid-Str. 5, ☎ 9750, IV-V
H Sonnenbichl, Adolf-Schmid-Str. 2, ☎ 78080, V-VI
H Bergfried, Adolf-Schmid-Str. 8, ☎ 78068, III-IV
H St. Peter, Luitpoldstr. 17, ☎ 96880, IV-V
H Sparkassenhotel, Luitpoldstr. 8, ☎ 7060, V
H Eisenrieth, Luitpoldstr. 23, ☎ 9610, II-IV
H Vier Jahreszeiten, Rinckstr. 1, ☎ 76770, V
H Dora, Frühlingstr. 12, ☎ 95880, III-IV
H Goldener Hirsch, Ludwigstr. 5, ☎ 4151, III
H Villa Schönblick, Tivolistr. 3, ☎ 78060, III-IV
H Traunfeldmühle, Traunfeldstr. 5, ☎ 98640, IV
H Villa Palmina, Mackstr. 4, ☎ 97660, IV-V
H Steiermark, Riedelstr. 4, ☎ 2962, III
Hg Moll, Frühlingstr. 61, ☎ 98680, III-IV
Hg Villa Rein, Frühlingstr. 8, ☎ 3482, V

Hg Rupertuspark, Friedrich-Ebert-Allee 66, ☎ 9850, IV-V
Hg Carola, Friedrich-Ebert-Allee, 6, ☎ 95840, IV-V ⌨
Hg Eva Maria, Zenostr. 2, ☎ 95390, II-IV
Hg Haus Lex, Salzburger Str. 42, ☎ 2147, II-III
P Haus Vroni, Paepkestr. 3, ☎ 5334, IV-V
P Hubertus, Am Thumsee 5, ☎ 2252, III-IV
P Villa Antonie, Traunfeldstr. 20, ☎ 2630, III
P Clematis, Frühlingstr. 6, ☎ 62593, II
P Haus Emmaus, Maximilianstr. 10, ☎ 78050, IV-V
P Villa Fischer, Adolf-Schmid-Str. 4, ☎ 5764, II
Pz Gästehaus Färber, Kirchholzstr. 1, ☎ 3462, III
Pz Gästehaus Geigl, Kirchholzstr. 3, ☎ 2270, II
Pz Gästehaus Mauerer, Ludwig-Thoma-Str. 9, ☎ 5517, III
Pz Haus Rachl, Salzburger Str. 44, ☎ 3641, II
Pz Jodlbauer, Bruchthal 15, ☎ 5152, II
Pz Haus Ronald, Frühlingstr. 67, ☎ 4433, I-II
Pz Schröder, Franz-Josef-Str. 4, ☎ 690020, II
Pz Kober, Franz-Josef-Str. 2, ☎ 769870, II-III

Nonn

H Gablerhof, Nonn 55, ☎ 98340, IV-V ⌨
H Sonnleiten, Nonn 27, ☎ 61009, V-VI
Gh Graue Katz, Nonn 20, ☎ 2144, II
P Schwarzenbach, Nonn 91, ☎ 4472, II-III
Pz Leitnerhof, Nonn 86, ☎ 8002, II
Pz Flatscherhof, Nonn 21, ☎ 8810, II

Marzoll Türk

Pz Gästehaus Scheil, Untersbergstr. 29, ☎ 8034, II-III

Bayerisch Gmain

Postal code: 83457; Tel. area code: 08651

🛈 Tourist-Info, Großgmainer Str. 14, ☎ 606401
H Amberger, Schiller Allee 5, ☎ 98650, III-IV ⌨
H Villa Florida, Grossgmainer. 23-25, ☎ 98880, III-IV ⌨

H Johanneshof, Unterbergstr. 6, ☎ 965860, II-IV
H Rupertus, Rupertistr. 3, ☎ 97820, V-VI
H Sonnenhof, Sonnenstr. 11, ☎ 959840, III
H Post, Bahnhofstr. 17, ☎ 98810, III-IV
Gh Bauerngirgl, Lattenbergstr. 19, ☎ 2625, III ⌨
Pz Karolinenhof, Weißbachstr. 19, ☎ 2811, II-III
Pz Schleicherhof, Harbacherstr. 5, ☎ 61716, II
Pz Gästehaus Bergfrieden, Taufkirchenweg 7, ☎ 4475, III
Pz Gästehaus Berghof, Bichlstr. 3, ☎ 3471, II
Pz Bräulerhof, Berchtesgadener Str. 60, ☎ 2923, II
Pz Gästhaus Dreher, Feuerwehrheimstr. 1, ☎ 65656, III
Pz Haus Forster, Müllnerhornstr. 3, ☎ 2642, II-III
Pz Haus Lug ins Land, Sonnenstr. 24, ☎ 95940, III-IV
Pz Streitbichlhof, Gruttensteinstr. 10, ☎ 8104, I-II
Pz Gästehaus Amadeus, Wappachweg 5, ☎ 2826, I-II
Bh Pflegerhof, Reichenhaller Str. 2, ☎ 3744, I-II

Bischofswiesen

Postal code: 83483; Tel. area code: 08652
🛈 Verkehrsamt, Hauptstr. 40, ☎ 977220

H Reissenlehen, Reissenpoint 11, ☎ 977200, V-VI
H Hundsreitlehen, Quellweg 11, ☎ 9860, IV-V
H Brennerbascht, Hauptstr. 44, ☎ 7021, III-IV
Gh Watzmannstube, Hauptstr. 16, ☎ 7223, II
P Loiplstüberl, Klemmsteinweg 12, ☎ 98480, II-III
P Huber Sepp, Pfaffenkogelweg 5, ☎ 7494, II-III
P Bergsicht, Keilhofgasse 33, ☎ 7393, II
P Weinbuch, Wassererweg 2, ☎ 7746, II
P Naglerlehen, Wiedlanerweg 7, ☎ 7166, II
P Reissenlehen, Reissenpoint 11, ☎ 977200, III
Pz Hasenknopf, Am Datzmann 91, ☎ 8554, II
Pz Gästehaus Sonja, Am Datzmann 71, ☎ 7769, II-III
Pz Gästehaus Marchler, Marchlerweg 10, ☎ 7782, II-III
Pz Haus Alpengruss, Reichenhaller Str. 26, ☎ 8414, KK
Pz Hillebrand, Am Hillebrand 10, ☎ 7098, II
Pz Fuchslechner, Wassererweg 19, ☎ 7108, II

Strub

Postal code: 83489; Tel. area code: 08652
P Watzmannblick, Gebirgsjägerstr. 46, ☎ 3363, II-III
P Haus Waldfrieden, Silbergstr. 50, ☎ 62964, II
⛺ Gebirgsjägerstr. 52, ☎ 94370 ⌨

Berchtesgaden

Postal code: 83471; Tel. area code: 08652
🛈 Berchtesgaden Tourismus GmbH, Königsseer Str. 2 , ☎ 9670
🛈 Tourismusbüro, Maximilianstr. 9, ☎ 9445300
🛈 Verkehrsbüro Oberau, Roßfeldstr. 22, ☎ 964960
H Bavaria, Sunklergässchen 11, ☎ 96610, V-VI

H Fischer, Königseestr. 51, ☎ 9550, V-VI
H Kronprinz, Am Brandholz, ☎ 6070, V-VI 🛏
H Wittelsbach, Maximilianstr. 16, ☎ 96380, IV-V
H Krone, Am Rad 5 1/3, ☎ 94600, V-VI
H Seimler, Maria am Berg 3, ☎ 6050, IV-V
H Binderhäusl, Am Wemholz 2, ☎ 5429, IV-V
H Lockstein, Am Lockstein 1, ☎ 2122, III
H Demming, Sunklergässchen 2, ☎ 9610, V-VI
H Hainberg, Waltenberger Str. 5, ☎ 62031, II-IV
H Grünberger, Hanserweg 1, ☎ 4560, V
H Vier-Jahreszeiten, Maximilianstr. 20, ☎ 9520, V-VI
H Weiherbach, Weiherbachweg 6, ☎ 978880, IV-VI
H Rosenbichl, Rosenhofweg 24, ☎ 94400, IV-V
Hg Floriani, Königseestr. 37, ☎ 66011, III-IV
Gh Schwabenwirt, Königsseer Str. 1, ☎ 2022, III-V
Gh Maria Gern, Kirchpl. 3, ☎ 3440, IV-V
Gh Mitterweinfeld, Weinfeldweg 6, ☎ 61374, II
Gh Deml, Bergwerkstr. 68, ☎ 61099, II-III
P Belvedere, Eberweinweg 1, ☎ 3573, II-III
P Rostalm, Rostwaldstr. 12, ☎ 3133, III-IV
P Haus Burgl, Renothenweg 27, ☎ 3980, II
P Grüßer, Hanserweg 1, ☎ 62609, I-II
P Achental, Ramsauerstr. 4, ☎ 4549, II-III
P Rubertiwinkel, Königsseer Str. 29, ☎ 4187, II-III
P Haus Gute Fahrt, Bergwerkstr. 24, ☎ 4739, II-III
P Villa Lockstein, Locksteinstr. 18, ☎ 61496, II
P Rennlehen, Rennweg 21, ☎ 66601, II-III
Pz Nagellehen, Locksteinstr. 33, ☎ 62505, II

Pz Weigl, Locksteinstr. 45, ☎ 4673, I-II
Pz Heidi, Weinfeldweg 9, ☎ 63734, II
Pz Etzerschlössl, Gernerstr. 2, ☎ 2882, II-III
Pz Schwabenbichl, Hansererweg 10, ☎ 690930, II 🛏
Pz Stollnhäusl, Königseer Str. 18, ☎ 63573, II 🛏
Pz Haus Brunner, Hansererweg 16, ☎ 61886, I
Pz Haus Sonnenblick, Kranzbichlweg 21, ☎ 3808, I 🛏
Pz Kilianmühle, Königsallee 2, ☎ 64292, II
Pz Kropfleiten, Metzenleitenweg 32, ☎ 3137, II-III

Stanggass

H Schönfeldspitze, Schönfeldspitzweg 8, ☎ 2349, III-IV
H Oberkälberstein, Oberkälberstein 25, ☎ 4539, III
P Edelweißstüberl, Zwingerstr. 7, ☎ 2237, I-II

Marktschellenberg

Postal code: 83487; Tel. area code: 08650
🛈 Verkehrsamt, Salzburger Str. 2, ☎ 988830
H Von der Albe, Marktplatz 7, ☎ 9889-0
Gh Zum Untersberg, Salzburger Str. 12, ☎ 244, III
P Doffenmühle, Nesseltalweg 11, ☎ 421, III
P Sonnhof, Alte Berchtesgadener Str. 2, ☎ 446,
P Haus Ehler, Gastagweg 9, ☎ 657, III

St. Leonhard

Postal code: 5083; Tel. area code: 06246
H Untersberg, Dr.-Friedrich-Oedl-Weg 1, ☎ 72575, V
Gh Schorn, St.-Leonhard-Str. 1, ☎ 72334, IV-V
Gh Simmerlwirt, St. Leonhardstr. 4, ☎ 72466, III
P Leonharderhof, Mitterweg 14, ☎ 72640, II
P Bergfried, Untersbergstr. 32, ☎ 73147, II

Bh Helenenhof, Drachenlochstr. 1a, ☎ 72330, II
Bh Grubergut, Mitterweg 16, ☎ 74611, I

Grödig

Postal code: 5082; Tel. area code: 06246
🛈 Gemeindeamt, Dr.-Richard-Hartmann-Str. 1,
  ☎ 72106-0
🛈 Tourismusverband, Gartenauerstr. 8, ☎ 73570
H Grödig, Neue-Heimat-Str. 15, ☎ 73523, II-IV
Gh Fürstenbrunn, Fürstenbrunner Str. 50, ☎ 73342, III
Gh Esterer, Glanstr. 31, ☎ 73321, V
Gh Racklwirt, Schützenstr. 25, ☎ 72267, II
Gh Schnöll, Marktstr. 8, ☎ 72223, II-IV
P Sallerhof, Hauptstr. 9, ☎ 72521, III-IV
P Bachmann, Bachmannweg 3, ☎ 72141, II-III
Pz Graggaber, Hauptstr. 34, ☎ 74099, I 🛏
Pz Helminger, Franz-Peyerl-Str. 2, ☎ 72538, I 🛏
Pz Hlawa, Marktstr. 7a, ☎ 77532, II
Bh Azetmüller, Eichetmühlweg 1, ☎ 72858, I 🛏
Bh Ulmhof, Neue-Heimat-Str. 14, ☎ 75862, I
Bh Ziegler, Bachmannweg 1, ☎ 72506, I-II

Anif

Postal code: 5081; Tel. area code: 06246
🛈 Verkehrsverein, Anif 31, ☎ 72365, 74325
H Friesacher, Anif 58, ☎ 8977, V-VI
H Schlosswirt, Anif 22, ☎ 72175, V-VI
Gh Husarenritt, Anif 47, ☎ 72354, II
P Gaberhell, Anif 305, ☎ 72073, III
P Schiessling, Anif 17, ☎ 72485, II

P Wiesenberger, Anif 160, ☎ 72454, II
Pz Harml, Anif 223, ☎ 72571, II
Pz Mayr, Anif 44, ☎ 72396, II

Index of place names